BEYOND MILE Z

BEYOND MILE ZERO

THE VANISHING
ALASKA HIGHWAY LODGE COMMUNITY

TEXT BY LILY GONTARD
PHOTOGRAPHS BY MARK KELLY

Additional photo captions: Front cover, from top, left to right—Alaska Highway sign in Dawson Creek; Forty-Mile Lodge; Lum 'n' Abner's, Silver Fox Road House; highway at Mile 1167; Jack Gunness at Double "G" Service; sign outside Tetsa River Lodge. Back cover, from top, left to right—Willy Lou Warbelow, photo courtesy Cyndie Warbelow-Tack and Art Warbelow; Border City Lodge & RV Park; Sid van der Meer; vintage coffee pot from Transport Café; Summit Lake Lodge; hat collection at Toad River Lodge; sign outside Fireside Inn; Rancheria Lodge. Page 1—The aurora and tail lights combine for a light show along the Alaska Highway. Previous pages—A lone sign marks the site of a former Alaska Highway lodge. Opposite—Linda and Denis Bouchard, Mile 710 Rancheria Lodge. Page 6—Sheep Mountain Motel has been nearly reclaimed by nature.

Lost Moose is an imprint of Harbour Publishing Co. Ltd.
P.O. Box 219, Madeira Park, BC, V0N 2H0
www.harbourpublishing.com

Edited by Joanna Reid
Indexed by Kyla Shauer
Cover design by Anna Comfort O'Keeffe
Text and map design by Roger Handling, Terra Firma Digital Arts
Epigraph, page 19 from "Say the Names" by Al Purdy, *Beyond Remembering: The Collected Poems of Al Purdy*, edited by Sam Solecki, 2000, Harbour Publishing.
Printed and bound in Canada

Harbour Publishing acknowledges the support of the Canada Council for the Arts, which last year invested $153 million to bring the arts to Canadians throughout the country. We also gratefully acknowledge financial support from the Government of Canada through the Canada Book Fund and from the Province of British Columbia through the BC Arts Council and the Book Publishing Tax Credit.

Library and Archives Canada Cataloguing in Publication
Gontard, Lily, author
　　　Beyond mile zero : the vanishing Alaska Highway lodge community / text by Lily Gontard ; photographs by Mark Kelly.
Includes index.
Issued in print and electronic formats.
ISBN 978-1-55017-797-8 (softcover).—ISBN 978-1-55017-798-5 (HTML)

　　　1. Hospitality industry—Alaska Highway—History—20th century. 2. Alaska Highway—History—20th century. I. Title.
FC4023.9.A4G66 2017　　　917.19'106　　　C2017-900657-6
　　　　　　　　　　　　　　　　　　　　　　　C2017-900658-4

This book is dedicated to all the people who have operated and worked in lodges along the Alaska Highway. Their hospitality and friendship, and help in times of need, have made the journey along the highway even more legendary, and often less scary.

We'd like to particularly thank Linda and Denis Bouchard, who run Mile 710 Rancheria Lodge. Linda and Denis were our first portraits and first interview for this project. Their generosity was the launching point, and we are deeply grateful.

"The hospitality of the people in the North is out of this world. In the early years you could go to any place, didn't matter, and you were welcome there—you might have to sleep on the floor."
Harry George (cited in *North to Alaska!* by Ken Coates)

CONTENTS

Preface   8

Introduction: "The Longest Main Street in North America"   18

1. Of Ghosts and Memories: Mile 0 to Mile 375 Tetsa River Lodge   34

2. Through the Mountains, across Streams and Rivers We Go: Mile 392 Summit Lake to Mile 463 Muncho Lake Lodge   65

3. The Liard River Corridor: Mile 496 Lower Liard River Lodge to Mile 620 Lower Post Lodge   94

4. The Lonely Road: Mile 596 Iron Creek Lodge to Mile 836.5 Johnson's Crossing   109

5. Is It Better to Be Bought Out or to Just Fade Away?: Mile 843 Silver Dollar to Mile 1093 Burwash Landing Resort   144

6. Toward the Border: Mile 1095 Joe's Airport to Mile 1220 Pioneer Inn   163

7. The End of the Line: Mile 1225.5 Border City Lodge & RV Park to Mile 1404.1 Silver Fox Roadhouse   196

Afterword: The End, but Is It Really *The End*?   232

Acknowledgements   234

Index   237

PREFACE

TRAVELLING FROM THE "lower forty-eight" states to Alaska, or from southern Canada to the Yukon and Northwest Territories, is a journey that most people do on the Alaska Highway. Sure, you can take the Alaska Marine Highway ferry along the West Coast to Skagway or Haines, Alaska, or the Cassiar Highway through British Columbia, but eventually, you'll end up on this historic road.

In the 1990s, Mark Kelly and I were both in our twenties when we moved (not together) to the North, and we each drove the Alaska Highway. My trip was made memorable by the first time I saw bison

Alaska Highway lodges, such as Double "G" Service, pictured, have traditionally offered fuel, food, accommodation and most importantly, tire-repair services.

near Liard Hot Springs Provincial Park, and by the fact that the windshield of the van I was travelling in was totally shattered by a rock that flew out of a dump truck just west of Teslin, Yukon.

Mark's first journey up the Alaska Highway was for a canoe trip on the Dease River. Years later, he transported his life from Squamish, British Columbia, to the Yukon and strapped to the roof of the truck was the same canoe he took on the Dease trip. In 2004, Liard Hot Springs Provincial Park became the background for that fateful moment when Mark fell in love with his future wife, Brooke, as they watched the northern lights wash in waves through a winter sky.

In the 1990s, fuel along the Alaska Highway was more expensive than in Edmonton or Dawson Creek, and both Mark and I travelled with a twenty-litre jerry can strapped to the roof racks of our respective vehicles. We both stopped for fuel only when necessary, and sometimes we'd stop at one of the lodges for a meal or coffee and a slice of pie. We share memories of the gas jockeys, wait staff and cashiers slightly tinged with a crustiness, and it's no wonder the service was less than enthusiastic: the 1990s saw the decline of the lodge community, after the heyday of the early 1980s.

For the most part, Alaska Highway lodge owners are a welcoming lot. Depending how long you stick around, you might get lucky and hear a tale or two.

The seed for *Beyond Mile Zero* was planted in late summer of 2011. Mark and Brooke's son, Seth, was born in July of that year, and shortly after his birth, the trio drove to Calgary to visit family. As parents know, a road trip with a newborn means frequent stops, and these occurred conveniently at abandoned lodges. While Brooke fed Seth, Mark would busy himself by taking photographs. It was Brooke who first suggested Mark do a photo essay on the changing highway lodge culture. Three years later, Mark asked me for advice about what to do with the growing collection of photos he'd taken of

abandoned Alaska Highway lodges. We met for coffee, and I said his photos would make a great book. But first, I thought I'd pitch a photo essay to *Geist*. That's how the feature "The Vanishing Roadhouse" ended up being published in Issue 100 in 2016.

Initially, the project centred around the abandoned lodges, the "fossils" of the highway lodge community: abandoned garages, piles of old tires, broken windows and peeling wallpaper. As we met more and more people who lived and worked along the highway, however, the story of the community emerged, and we began to uncover a hidden history.

During our first research road trip in August 2015, Mark and I drove from Whitehorse, Yukon, to Delta Junction, Alaska, with a current issue of *The Milepost*—the travel bible for the route, published annually since 1949—and two lists of Alaska Highway lodges from 1947 and 1948. We wanted to see which lodges were still around. We found that most of the lodges no longer existed, and that there were lodges on the highway that weren't on the list. We expanded our scope.

The author, on a research road trip, stops for refreshment at Pine Valley Bakery and Lodge.

Our first interview on that 2015 road trip was with Ben Zhu, who co-manages Kluane Park Inn (KPI) with his parents, Gary and Sue. The family are recent arrivals to the Yukon, and they're obviously loving it. The Zhus moved from Vancouver to run a lodge in Haines Junction, a small remote community in the Yukon. They represented a new kind of lodge owner: city folk who'd moved to the country.

In the bar of the KPI (which is legendary for raucous parties and good times), we met Ollie and Helen

Wirth, who owned Burwash Landing Resort for thirty-one years. Both were nostalgic about their years operating the lodge—recalling community events such as curling bonspiels, the mad rush of seventeen tour buses that would stop in for lunch—and expressed their disappointment that the new owner, the economic branch of Kluane First Nation, closed the lodge in 2013 instead of continuing the legacy. The lodge was opened in 1947 by the Jacquot brothers and, until 2013, was one of the longest continually operating lodges along the highway.

After talking with the Wirths, we knew there was more to the stories of the highway lodges than the day-to-day mechanics of running a business. People arrived at lodge ownership through direct or circuitous routes: the Porsilds from Denmark via the Canadian Arctic, Sid van der Meer from Holland via Alberta and the Scoby family from Michigan straight to Alaska. These people were intimately connected to the places where they lived, raised children, made friends, and succeeded and failed.

Mark and I started working together on this project in December 2014. And, including his trip in 2011, altogether, we took five road trips and drove 8,113 kilometres (5,041 miles). That's nearly four times the length of the Alaska Highway. We conducted more than forty interviews and took more than five thousand photographs. We talked with lodge owners along the Alaska Highway, and we tracked down former lodge owners who had retired to Oregon and Fairbanks. So many of the original lodge owners have passed away, but we found their children who had grown up at the lodges, and they live in Georgia, British Columbia, and Yukon. We conducted interviews via email, telephone and Skype. We did all this at the same time as we worked our full-time "paying" jobs. We know there remains more to discover, but we tried to capture as much as we could.

Mark and I are interested in people's stories. As a photographer, he is looking for the story that gives mood and composition to a photograph. As a writer, I am inspired by the stories of everyday life and a desire to interpret, shape and share them with others. The stories we heard propelled us constantly forward, pushing us to do one more photo shoot or one more interview, to make one more telephone call.

When we started our project, we had very few expectations, aside from eating homemade pie and other baked goods. We found far more than we anticipated. We met people who were willing to share their time with us and tell us about their lives. Lodge owners are an unusual bunch. Free spirits, they set up businesses, for the most part, under challenging circumstances in the middle of nowhere. The stories of how and why they arrived, stayed and left are varied and compelling.

The people we met share common characteristics: they are mavericks, entrepreneurs; they are independent, creative. They all share an adventurous spirit and are resourceful in the way they address their challenges, solve problems and create a community. The people

Barbara Abbott runs Tundra Lodge and RV Park in Tok, Alaska. The RV park's bar used to be Rita's Roadhouse, which was moved from the east side of the village to its present location in the 1960s.

who first started the lodges were self-sufficient, pioneers in aviation, in outfitting, in tourism. The modern world of automation, instant communication and government legislation has obliterated the conditions that allowed those lodge owners to experiment—for example, learning how to fly a plane by purchasing one, starting the engine and taxiing down the highway. These people are part of an era that we'll not see again.

Help us grow the history

We know we didn't include all the lodges and all the stories in this book, but we're always looking for more. Contact us on our social media channels to tell us know about lodges that weren't listed on the map in this book, or to share your stories and memories:

Twitter: @BeyondMile0

Facebook: www.Facebook.com/BeyondMile0

A Note on Measurements of Distance

When the Alaska Highway was built, both Canada and the United States used the imperial system for measurements (though a US gallon remained inexplicably larger than a Canadian one). After Canada adopted the White Paper on Metric Conversion in 1970, the country slowly began the switch to the metric system. But Canadians have never fully embraced the metric system and navigate using a comfortable middle ground: recipes, weight and height are most commonly measured in imperial, whereas distance and fuel are measured in metric.

Almost three quarters of the Alaska Highway (or "ALCAN Highway," as it is often called) passes through Canada. In Canada, the mileposts and imperial distance signs on the Alaska Highway were removed in the late 1970s, replaced with distance signs and markers in kilometres. Lodges along the Alaska Highway have traditionally been identified by the milepost where they stand, and lodge owners

Though officially the Alaska Highway starts at Mile 0, Dawson Creek, British Columbia, prior to its construction there was a pre-existing road between Dawson Creek and just north of Fort St. John, to Charlie Lake.

and truckers commonly speak about distance in historic miles. For the sake of this tradition, distances in this book will be measured in miles.

Another tricky point about distances on the Alaska Highway is that originally this route was 1,422 miles long, but after years of roadwork, it has been straightened and shortened. Its current total length is an elastic number that hovers around 1,387 miles. At the Alaska-Yukon border, distance markers challenge the driver, as there is a 35-mile difference between the actual distance from Dawson Creek, British Columbia, and the number on mileposts. Although the official end point is Mile 1422 Delta Junction, Alaska, the common misperception is that the end lies 96 miles farther northwest, at Fairbanks.

While reading this book, if you are able, suspend your belief in the superiority of the metric system and the simple power of dividing by ten, as well as even a need for accurate measurement. And, for those of you who have a hard time thinking in miles, just remember: 1 mile is equal to 1.6 kilometres.

The original Mile 0 milepost stands proudly in the middle of a major intersection in the centre of Dawson Creek, British Columbia.
Yukon Archives, Rolf and Margaret Hougen fonds. 2010/91, #1005. Photo by Rolf Hougen, 1946.

THE ALASKA HIGHWAY

Fairbanks

Delta Junction

Dot Lake

ALASKA

Tok

Tetlin Junction

Northway
Junction

Beaver Creek

1

Anchorage

Burwash Landing   Destructi

Haines Junct

CANADA
USA

CANADA
USA

COMMUNITIES OF THE ALASKA HIGHWAY

Mile 35 Taylor

Mile 47 Fort St. John

Mile 52 Charlie Lake

Mile 101 Wonowon

Mile 140 Pink Mountain

Mile 233 Prophet River

Mile 300 Fort Nelson

Mile 422 Toad River

Mile 456 Muncho Lake

Mile 620 Lower Post

Mile 635 Watson Lake

Mile 804 Teslin

Mile 918 Whitehorse

Mile 974 Champagne

Mile 1016 Haines Junction

Mile 1083 Destruction Bay

Mile 1093 Burwash Landing

Mile 1202 Beaver Creek

Mile 1264 Northway Junction

Mile 1280 Tanacross

Mile 1306 Tetlin Junction

Mile 1314 Tok

Mile 1361 Dot Lake

Mile 1422 Delta Junction

PACIFIC OCEAN

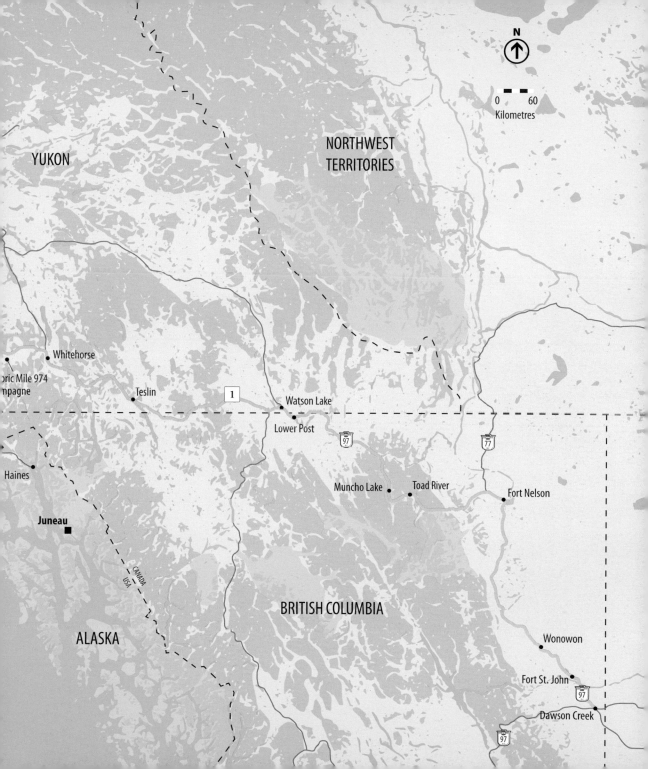

INTRODUCTION

"THE LONGEST MAIN STREET IN NORTH AMERICA"

"till the heart stops beating / say the names"
Al Purdy

Silver Tip, Rocky Mountain, Swift River, Silver Dollar, Pink Mountain, Steamboat, Prophet River, Toad River, Krak-a-Krik—the names of lodges along the Alaska Highway read like a list of fairy tale place names. As you drive from Mile Zero at Dawson Creek, British Columbia, to the northern terminus at Mile 1,422 Delta Junction, Alaska, you can see many of these lodges—unofficial monuments to road travel—some of which evolved from the camps for the US Army crews who built the highway in 1942 or the camps that remained for road maintenance into the 1960s, and beyond.

However, sometimes you have to pull over and stop the car, open the door, and walk past the trees and shrubs that creep toward the soft shoulder and border the ditch. What hides from view is the slow degeneration of the lodge community that in its heyday was known as "the longest Main Street in North America." Off the side of the highway, in the woods or in plain sight, will lie a log or frame structure partially demolished, with paint peeling from the walls, the vinyl seating and the wood panelling of sixties or seventies decor. Exterior and interior walls painted Caribbean blue or Smartie purple or seafoam green. Sloppy and expanding smears of garbage. Long gone are the Saturday night dances, the curling bonspiels that livened up the winter days, the miles-long drives to drop in for a cup of coffee. The busy sounds of an entrepreneurial community that began more than seventy years ago are now barely a hum on the landscape.

Opposite: Cook's Koidern, pictured, was operated by Jim and Dorothy Cook for decades and has been closed since 2015.

BUILDING THE HIGHWAY

IN THE EARLY 1940s, most of the world was deeply entrenched in the manoeuvres of World War II. The eastern shores of North America were endangered by secretive German U-boats gliding stealthily through and by open navy battles on the Atlantic Ocean. From across the Pacific, Japan threatened from the west; it trounced its adversaries in the South Pacific and, in June 1942, overtook the Attu and Kiska Islands in the Aleutians, an Alaskan archipelago that gently curves across the Bering Sea toward Asia. The Americans supposed that this string of islands presented an easy route by which the Japanese might choose to invade Alaska and gain access to the continent.

Ultimately, it was the attack on Pearl Harbor in Hawaii, on December 7, 1941, that set in motion one of the greatest highway construction challenges of the twentieth century. It was in this military theatre—North America facing adversaries on both coasts—that the Alaska Military Highway was built to facilitate the movement of troops to the undefended and sparsely populated northwestern frontier of the United States: Alaska. In March 1942, US Army Corps of Engineers (USACE) troops from the "lower forty-eight" states started arriving in northern Canada and Alaska to build a winding pioneer road; it was surveyed from Dawson Creek, British Columbia, north through the Yukon Territory, and then northwest, ending in Big Delta at the confluence of the Tanana and Delta Rivers in Alaska.

In 1942, very few people lived along what would become the Alaska Highway corridor. The area of British Columbia from Dawson Creek to the Yukon border was sparsely populated, with a concentration of about five hundred in Dawson Creek. The Yukon counted just shy of five thousand people living within the territory's borders, and Alaska had a population of seventy-four thousand, mostly found

Opposite: Mile 1061 Soldier's Summit celebrates the end of the construction of the Alaska Highway in October 1942 when the last two sections were joined. However, the celebratory plaque is far from the location where the completion actually took place, which is closer to Mile 1202 Beaver Creek, Yukon.
"Alaska Highway" © Government of Canada, reproduced with permission of Library and Archives Canada (2016). Library and Archives Canada / Department of National Defence fonds / e010781534.

along the coast. Local people were hired for the construction, but the bulk of the work fell to a workforce that included ten thousand–plus American soldiers and six thousand civilians.

Until the construction of the Alaska Highway, the US Army did not allow racially segregated units to work alongside non-segregated units, and with the latter engaged in the war effort outside of the United States, the army was forced to change its policy if it wanted to complete this gargantuan project. The construction of the Alaska Highway became an equalizing event for the US Army as that country was heading toward the 1950s and 1960s, decades that would see the civil rights movement finally bring an end to government-sanctioned segregation policies. As John Virtue explains in his book

The Black Soldiers Who Built the Alaska Highway, the construction of the highway would be the first time that US Army soldiers worked together no matter the colour of their skin. Despite collaborating on the project as a whole, the army units worked independently of one another on their respective sections of the highway, and there is much anecdotal evidence that segregated units were provided with inferior supplies and charged with developing the more difficult sections of the highway.

Initial construction of the highway was completed in late October 1942, when Private Alfred Jalufka of Kennedy, Texas, of the USACE 18th Regiment, driving a bulldozer northwest, and Corporal Refines Sims Jr., from Philadelphia, Pennsylvania, of the USACE 97th (a segregated regiment), driving a bulldozer southeast from Alaska, met in the middle of a dense spruce forest near Beaver Creek, on the Canadian side of the border.

The original highway was called a "corduroy" road, referring to the way the road surface was constructed: tree trunks were laid down and covered with earth. This type of road made for a reverberating driving experience. However, when the route was finished, it was barely drivable in some sections and contractors working for the US Bureau of Public Roads had to regrade, reroute and redo the highway. Although the highway has been paved and chip-sealed from end to end, there are sections that continue to be improved—curves straightened, narrow sections widened, bulging frost heaves flattened out—even to this day.

The Alaska section of the highway was handed over to the Alaska Road Commission in 1944, but the US Army remained in charge of the Canadian part until April 1, 1946, when it was handed over to the Royal Canadian Engineers (RCE). Keeping the roadway in a drivable condition required constant maintenance, such as grading, repairing bridges and fixing the roadway after washouts, by the Northwest Highway Maintenance Establishment, which worked under the direction of the RCE.

When the US Army constructed the pioneer road, it also installed a long-distance pole-line communication system along the highway, but no power lines were added. This decision would have a big impact on highway lodges, as it would force them to rely on generators for power, and the cost of fuel would influence all pricing, from a cup of coffee to the price of a room. After World War II, Canadian National Telecommunications camps were established at the repeater stations to maintain the communications network along the highway. These camps, such as the one at Summit, British Columbia, became small communities consisting of their staff, the highway crews and their families.

Once initial construction of the highway was completed and the US Army moved out of the North, surveyors, heavy-equipment operators and mechanics were still needed, as were administrators, who

Opposite: Mile 717.5
Message Post Lodge
was open until the late
1980s and according
to *The Milepost*, the
lodge offered "food,
gas, a beer garden and
souvenirs."

were necessary to control the immense task of managing mainte-nance and care of the highway. This demand led to an increase in the number of women working along the highway, who during the construction phase had held only one of every twenty-four jobs, mostly in administrative support and service positions. This "one in twenty-four" number comes from a website created jointly by Yukon Tourism and Culture, Archives Canada and Canadian Heri-tage, called The Alaska Highway: A Yukon Perspective.

THE FIRST LODGES

In the 1950s Lum 'n' Abner's was owned by Mr. and Mrs. Arthur Boyes.

Yukon Archives, Rolf and Margaret Hougen fonds, 2010/91, #1024. Photo by Rolf Hougen, 1946.

UNTIL THE CONSTRUCTION of the Alaska Highway, trains and riverboats were the primary modes of transportation in the Yukon and Alaska. There was a railway line from Skagway, Alaska, to Whitehorse, Yukon, and the Alaska Railroad owned several shorter railway lines that were eventually linked up. The White Pass and Yukon Route (WPYR) had a monopoly over the rail and river trans-portation from Skagway, Alaska, into the miner-al-rich Yukon Territory. After the road was built, WPYR's subsidiary, the British Yukon Navigation Company (BYNC), provided bus services between Dawson Creek, British Columbia, and Scottie Creek, Alaska. Over the years, this bus company built sev-eral lodges to accommodate its passengers: Fort Nel-son Hotel and a lodge in Lower Post, both in British Columbia, and Dry Creek Lodge and Koidern Lodge in the Yukon Territory. An interpretive panel com-memorating Mile 710 Rancheria Lodge as the first BYNC lodge construction to open on the highway between Watson Lake and Whitehorse, Yukon, in 1946, describes the variation of early accommodations: "Hastily converted army

Opposite: The Alaska Military Highway was officially opened in November 1942. Though bus service was provided to military personnel and contractors throughout the 1940s, the highway was only opened to the public in 1948. Liard Lodge (pictured) was one of the first lodges constructed to accommodate bus traffic.
Yukon Archives, Rolf and Margaret Hougen fonds, 2010/91, (top) #463, (bottom) #1032. Photos by Rolf Hougen, 1946.

barrack buildings, stout two-story log structures and a framed wall tent for serving lunches."

But even with transportation services in place and burgeoning infrastructure, the promise of allowing tourists free rein over the length of the former military highway didn't come to fruition. Travellers still needed a permit and had to prove that they had necessary supplies for the journey. Then with the opening of the highway to public traffic in 1948, more lodges sprouted up to provide meals, services and accommodations to people working on and travelling along the highway.

Since the highway opened to the public, lodges have opened and closed, such as Mile 233 Lum 'n' Abner's and Mile 1095 Joe's Airport, or lodges have opened, closed and then reopened, such as Mile 836.5 Johnson's Crossing and Mile 1147 Pine Valley Lodge. The businesses were built for the convenience of highway travellers and sold or abandoned by their owners when times got tough or it was simply time to move on. According to *The Milepost*, in 1955, services were available every 25 miles. The 2016 edition, meanwhile, advised travellers to watch the fuel gauge, as services were found at times only every 100 to 150 miles.

A WORLD OF VISITORS

BY THE TIME THE ALASKA HIGHWAY opened to the public, people were chomping at the bit to drive this road and explore the northwest reaches of North America. The Alaska Highway Heritage Project website notes that in 1948 tourists driving the highway numbered 18,600, and a mere three years later that number jumped to 50,000. The recent number, from Yukon Tourism border crossing statistics for 2015, may come as a surprise: 327,778. There's no denying the attraction of driving the fabled road.

Back in the summer of 1943, when travel on the highway was only allowed for military purposes and residents, Mrs. Gertrude Tremblay Baskine from Toronto, Ontario, arrived in the Canadian commissioner's office in Edmonton, Alberta, determined to acquire an Alaska Military Highway Permit. The permit was an elusive and mysterious piece of paper that would give Gertrude access to the ALCAN from Mile 0 in Dawson Creek, British Columbia, to the end, at Mile 1,422 in Big Delta, Alaska. Why did she want to travel the highway? Her reason was simple: "It was impossible, naturally I had to try it."

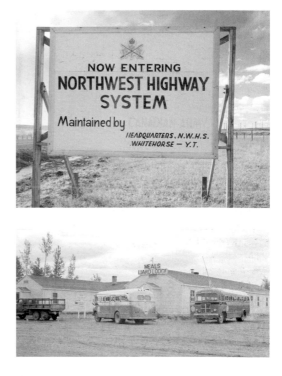

By this time in her career, Gertrude had achieved a number of things she'd set her mind to: she had a degree in social work from McGill University and a master's from Columbia University, and was a graduate in letters from the Sorbonne University in Paris. She had worked as a social worker and a journalist. And in 1943, as a member of the Association of Canadian Clubs, she was travelling across Canada lecturing on the importance of women becoming involved in politics.

In her travel memoir *Hitch-Hiking the Alaska Highway*, Gertrude briefly mentions that Mr. Baskine fully supported her work (which turned out to be adventurous), but it's also reasonable to guess that she was well placed in higher society by birth and/or by marriage (most likely both), and had access to influential people and the necessary funds to finance her journey. Travel in the North has always been expensive, and was even more so in the 1940s. To get her Alaska

Memorabilia from the Alaska Highway construction days can be found at lodges, RV parks and in peoples' backyards from Dawson Creek, British Columbia, to Delta Junction, Alaska.

Military Highway Permit, Gertrude had to prove that she would not be a financial burden to the US Army.

In the summer of 1943, travel on the Alaska Highway was tightly controlled by the US Army, travel permits were inspected at military checkpoints, and only approved vehicles and people could travel the highway. It was seen as a virtually impossible act for a woman to travel the Alaska Military Highway—let alone on her own. (In fact, just after Gertrude left Dawson Creek, she heard that the army was going to ban women from travelling on the highway. So she put as much distance between herself and Dawson Creek as she could, as fast as she could.) But somehow, Gertrude left Edmonton with her permit in hand and set off to become the first and only woman to hitchhike the full length of the infamous roadway before it was opened to the public in 1948.

One year after her great adventure, Gertrude's memoir was published. The word "hitchhiking" is a bit misleading: Gertrude was courteously shuttled by a variety of trucks, cars and Jeeps from one construction camp to the other "up the line." Many people who worked on the construction of the highway had previously worked on the railway lines, and terminology from the railways permeated the highway lexicon. She even did a stint on horseback. She never actually put out her thumb, though she did get stuck in certain places for uncertain amounts of time, as hitchhikers so often do.

Gertrude travelled during wartime, and one of the restrictions on the publication of her memoir was that she wasn't allowed to name the military people she met or the military posts where she stopped.

However, she did mention the names of some construction and maintenance camps where she stayed: Mile 836.5 Johnson's Crossing, near where the Teslin River flows out of Teslin Lake, and Mile 1094 Burwash Landing, on the shore of Kluane Lake. Both Yukon camps later became the sites of well-known highway lodges.

In 2017, seventy-four years after Gertrude Tremblay Baskine made her memorable journey, there is hardly any record of her expedition or even her writing career. The McGill University Archives holdings are limited, and deep in the Pickering/Ajax digital archive there is an announcement in the November 1943 issue of *The Commando* for a presentation on December 5 by Gertrude, but little else.

LODGE CULTURE TODAY

KNOWLEDGEABLE AND COMFORTING, with the occasional cantankerous encounter, the Alaska Highway lodge community provides conversation and provisions in the middle of nowhere. The accommodations may be immaculately clean, at times slightly dated, the sheets a bit worn, but you can usually get a tire patched or a fuel tank filled. These days, most lodges have Wi-Fi; because cellphone service is still pretty much only available close to major cities, access to the World Wide Web is almost a necessity for the modern-day traveller. Often, you can tuck into a slice of homemade pie while posting to your social media accounts or checking email and road conditions.

Fresh baking and homestyle cooking are characteristic of the highway lodge culinary experience. At some point, cinnamon buns became the baked treat associated with the route, and lodge cooks bake these by the pan-load to satisfy the traveller's appetite. North of Fort Nelson, British Columbia, at Mile 375 Tetsa River Lodge, Ben and Gail Andrews bake up to three hundred cinnamon buns a day. Tetsa cinnamon buns are known for a light texture, a sprinkling of

nuts and a sweet glaze with a slightly salty taste that will make you buy a second one.

North of Tetsa River Lodge, Donna Rogers, who owns Mile 533 Coal River Lodge & RV in British Columbia, with her husband, Brent, also bakes cinnamon buns. But from the shelves in her restaurant you can also buy homemade preserves and chocolates, and in 2003, she received a postcard extolling the virtues of her bumbleberry pie from a fan in the United States who'd driven the length of the Alaska Highway. "She wrote that it was the best bumbleberry pie she'd tasted," Donna said.

Even though husband-and-wife teams have run lodges since the 1940s, official business partnerships pre-1980 consisted mostly of the husband and another man; the wife was not included on the paperwork. The labour at lodges was (and often continues to be) divided along traditional gender lines: the wife/woman takes care of the baking, cooking, cleaning and restaurant operations, while the husband/man runs the mechanical side of the operation, including the gas station and repair shop.

However, as is often the case in remote areas, traditional gender roles get thrown out the window when there's no one to do the work or when one person happens to be good at and simply enjoys work that's not traditionally associated with their gender. Siblings Ellen Davignon (née Porsild) and Aksel Porsild (whose parents, Bob and Elly, built Mile 836.5 Johnson's Crossing Lodge in the late 1940s) say that after running the restaurant in the morning, Elly would take a Swede saw and cut kindling for one hour every afternoon, even though there were plenty of able-bodied men or boys around who could do that work. At Mile 436.5 Double "G" Service, Jack Gunness, a tall burl of a man serves up slices of his home-baked bread almost as big as dinner plates.

On a highway lodge menu, you'll find a breakfast fry-up of eggs and a side of bacon, sausage or ham, with home baking, and soup made from scratch, along with deep-fried offerings and burgers. Vegetarians may be hard-pressed to find a tofu-, lentil- or bean-based dish, but there's probably an iceberg lettuce salad dressed with pale chopped tomatoes. Whatever you choose from the menu, there's always either water-weak or turpentine-strong coffee to wash it all down.

In fact, along this highway, where clean drinking water has at times been hard to come by, coffee was once the staple drink of lodge life. Gertrude Baskine recalled that in 1943, on the tables in the maintenance camp messes she visited, pots of coffee were replenished over and over, but no jug of water could be found. She felt she was being "weaned off drinking water" because she was told it was considered unsafe, since filtration and plumbing hadn't been installed at the camps where she stayed.

At Mile 836.5, which had been a military construction camp, the US Army made several unsuccessful drilling attempts for water so that access to it wouldn't be at the mercy of the freeze-up in winter. The Porsild family opened the Johnson's Crossing Lodge on the site in 1949, and for many years afterwards, they hauled water in a tank on a trailer from Brook's Brook maintenance camp six miles east down the highway. In the early 1950s, Bob Porsild installed a waterline from the river to the lodge, which was only used in the summer months. Water continued to be hauled from Brook's Brook over the fall and winter for several years.

Luckily, in the twenty-first century, drinking water along the highway is not such a rare commodity as in 1943. The majority of lodges have wells. Mile 533 Coal River Lodge & RV is near the confluence of the Coal and Liard Rivers, and Donna Rogers is particularly proud of the taste of the water from her well. She serves a glass as if she were pouring from an expensive bottle of grand cru wine.

Three things are necessary for lodges to operate: fuel, water and human power. Anything that affects the availability of those, influences whether a lodge can operate for another month, season or year.

Today, when you drive the Alaska Highway, for every lodge that is open and offering hospitality and conversation, you'll see one or two or three that are abandoned or have a *For Sale* sign posted on the property. If you look closely at the ground, you might see the outlines of old foundations. Sometimes, though, not even a trace remains: it could be that every hint of the lodge has disappeared, burned to the ground or been scavenged and carted away. The boom time of the highway lodges has passed, and what remains is a legend frayed on the edges.

Memory is reliant on perspective and experience, making history a malleable concept, and the histories of some Alaska Highway lodges are easier to unearth than others. Memoirs exist, and there are descendants and friends who recall stories, with or without embellishment. Meanwhile, other lodges are recorded solely as names in a single edition of a guidebook or map, the owners known or unknown, the stories evaporated into the landscape like the buildings that have been bulldozed or reclaimed by nature.

The Alaska Highway lodge community has evolved and devolved over time. Reliant on the highway traffic for its existence, the vitality of the community has been at the mercy of factors beyond its control, such as the "Black Monday" stock market crash of 1987 and the explosion of the American housing bubble of 2008, or the boom-and-bust nature of the oil and gas industry. The people who chose to open and/or operate highway lodges had to find within themselves the skills and resources to withstand outside forces, and continue to thrive, or not, whatever the case may have been. *Beyond Mile Zero* explores Alaska Highway lodges by sharing the unknown stories of a community that provides essential services along what remains a long and sometimes lonesome highway—a community that has been largely ignored by historians and journalists in favour of the hero-making effort that was the construction of the Alaska Highway.

Early lodges were built using available materials such as the spindly spruce trees of the boreal forest. Yukon Archives, Rolf and Margaret Hougen fonds, 2010/91, #1008. Photo by Rolf Hougen, 1946.

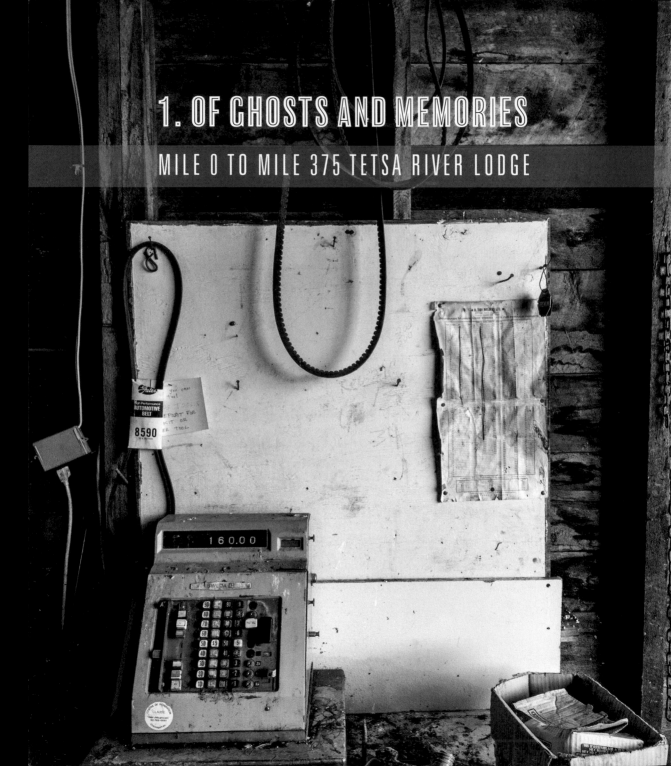

1. OF GHOSTS AND MEMORIES

MILE 0 TO MILE 375 TETSA RIVER LODGE

Mile 72 The Shepherd's Inn **1**
Mile 101 Blueberry
Mile 143 Pink Mountain Campsite and RV Park **2**
Mile 143 Pink Mountain Motor Inn / Buffalo Inn
Mile 144 Sasquatch Crossing Lodge
Mile 147 Beatton River / Tucker Inn
Mile 162 Sikanni Chief
Mile 171 Mason Creek
Mile 175 Buckinghorse River Lodge **3**
Mile 200 Trutch Lodge **4**
Mile 233 Prophet River / Lum 'n' Ahner's **5**
Mile 275 Hilltop
Mile 295.5 Auto Service
Mile 351 Steamboat Mountain **6**
Mile 363 Silver Tip Lodge
Mile 375 Tetsa River Lodge **7**

D awson Creek, British Columbia, is a city with a population of eleven thousand–plus that is just west of the border with the province of Alberta and 739 miles north of the city of Vancouver. Highway 49 approaches Dawson Creek from the east, and Highway 97 from the west, and just a few miles northwest of where these two highways meet, you'll find Mile 0 of the Alaska Highway: the start of the route north.

At the beginning of the twentieth century, the area around Dawson Creek was known as the Pouce Coupe Prairie, a name said to be derived from that of Chief Pouskapie (sometimes spelled

Opposite: Abandoned Mile 351 Steamboat was burned down not long after this photo was taken.

Pooscapee) of the Beaver First Nation. The Beaver and Cree First Nations had been living in the region for centuries, with a constant

rivalry between them and the Unjegah River (Peace River) dividing their territories. The prairie included present-day Pouce Coupe, Rolla and Dawson Creek. Just about every Dawson in Canada is named after George Mercer Dawson, the legendary surveyor, geologist and scientist from Nova Scotia.

The first Europeans found their way into the region in the late 1700s, and they were followed by the European fur traders. By 1891, the first settlers—members of the Thomas family (an anglicized version of "Tomas"), who were Métis—had begun farming. Then, in the late 1800s, came the large inmigration of non–First Nations people who were trying to take the extremely difficult overland route from Edmonton to the Klondike gold rush.

In 1912, the Canadian government put parcels of land for homesteading for sale, prompting the growth of a non–First Nations population in the region around Dawson Creek. A post-war land offer was made to veteran British subjects, and that increased even more the settler population of the hamlet of Dawson Creek. When the Northern Alberta Railway line came to halt a few miles east of the hamlet in 1931, community members slowly moved to be closer to the depot. By 1936, the population was just over five hundred, and the village of Dawson

Creek became incorporated. Then, in 1942, everything changed, as the US Army, very friendly-like, invaded the town. The construction of the Alaska Highway began. It wasn't long, though, before people began to see the potential for the highway after the war: tourism, travel, trade. If people were travelling up that rough road into the North, they would need services.

Soon after the end of the war, public transportation companies such as Canadian Coachways and the British Yukon Navigation Company fulfilled the mutual needs of their own businesses and highway travellers by building lodges that provided accommodation, meals, fuel and vehicle repairs. (Fuel companies later jumped in on the action too.) In some cases, prospective lodge owners could lease or buy a property and pay back what they owed to the company for a few cents on every gallon of fuel sold.

The BYNC, which had been busing people up and down the highway between Whitehorse and Dawson Creek under contract with the military, constructed lodges to serve its customers and hired people to run these businesses. Mile 710 Rancheria Lodge, built in 1946, was one of those lodges, and the first managers, Bud and Doris Simpson, ended up taking over ownership of the lodge and running it for thirty years. There was anticipation that the highway would be opened to tourists imminently, but it remained closed for more than two more years; a military permit was still required for travel.

Finally, the highway opened to the public in 1948. To coincide with the anticipated influx of tourists, on February 16, 1948, the Canadian Department of Mines and Resources published a list of available accommodations and roadside facilities. There were some free campgrounds, but accommodations were scarce. Of the lodges included in that list, only Mile 710 Rancheria and Mile 533 Coal River still operate today (though the buildings at Coal River are not the originals, most of which were burned to the ground in a fire in 1969).

Opposite top: Many of the entrepreneurs who started lodges along the Alaska Highway in the 1940s made use of the army and construction buildings left behind, such as the snow load–shedding Quonset hut.
Yukon Archives, Bloomstrand Family fonds, 98/73, #18.

Bottom: Mile 106 in 1948—Alaska Highway lodge culture was born of an era of unpaved roads and slower, less fuel-efficient vehicles.
Yukon Archives, Elmer Harp Jr. 2006/2, #17.

MILE 72 THE SHEPHERD'S INN

NORTH OF FORT ST. JOHN, at Mile 72, lies the Shepherd's Inn—a modern-looking building, clad in vinyl siding. Behind it, homes are neatly arranged with a suggestion of a communal feeling. The gas pumps are new, the restaurant bright. On the menu is standard diner fare (burgers, Caesar salad), but it's the homemade pies listed on a chalkboard on glass-fronted double-door fridges that are the stand-out items. Depending on the day and season, the selection could include berry medley, apple or pumpkin, or all three.

Opposite: The Shepherd's Inn is an unusual business along the Alaska Highway, as it's run by a non-denominational religious society, the Shepherd's Christian Society, and the business supports the adjacent community.

The air in the inn resounds with positivity, and the thirtysomething general manager, Ryan Hotston, and his octogenarian predecessor, Don Rutherford, are friendly and open in their approach to strangers. The non-denominational Shepherd's Christian Society purchased the property in 1982 after the previous owners went bankrupt, hence the name "The Shepherd's Inn." These founders had been living at a religious community farther north and decided they needed to move to a property where they could be self-sufficient. They knew nothing about running a service industry business; they opened the inn with "a belief that God would take care of us," says Don.

The Shepherd's Inn "opened its doors with a bunch of rank amateurs to run the place, with no experience," he says, his words lively with laughter. "All we had was a high hope that it was going to go—sometimes you have to make a sacrifice when you're starting something."

The on-grid community of about forty people lives on twelve hectares (thirty acres). It supplies its own water from three wells and grows its own food in greenhouses and gardens; unfortunately, that garden-fresh produce is used to feed the community and not the inn's guests. The inn includes a restaurant, a "C-store" (convenience store) and a twenty-four-room motel.

"Our church building is behind the restaurant and everyone that lives here is part of the community," says Ryan. "There's a school, church, the business, and the community is private. Not everybody can live there."

"There are about twenty people employed, mostly full-time," says Ryan. The majority of the staff is from the community. "Some of the seniors that live here are part time, and we're open all year round."

Staffing has been a constant challenge, because the inn is twenty-five miles from Fort St. John, which is a long commute for someone earning minimum wage ($10.55 an hour in BC). The Shepherd's Christian Society is committed to the long-term viability of its community and the business that supports it.

"The vision is to provide work for the members of the community—

Don Rutherford (right) managed the Shepherd's Inn with his wife, Dorothea. In 2016, Ryan Hotston (left) took over as the manager and is looking to the future of the business and the community it supports.

whether they be older or younger," says Ryan. "I have five children and when they're old enough, they'll be working here."

Ryan previously worked in the oil and gas industry and took over as the inn's general manager in May 2016, though he'd been in training since the previous January. His predecessor, Don, an accountant, was involved in the Shepherd's Inn from the very beginning: June 29, 1982. When Don became the general manager, his wife, Dorothea Mae, worked right alongside him.

Don is a consummate host; Ryan is friendly yet more reserved. Don smiles broadly with each statement he makes, and he takes the time to listen to questions. When he drifts off topic, he redirects his answers to the question that was originally asked. He was either born to welcome people to an establishment or he learned the skills of hosting during the decades he managed the inn.

"When things were quiet, people would come in and hug my wife," Don says. "We never had an argument at work for thirty years. It was not quite so peaceful at home."

"She was well liked," Ryan adds. "She made sure to ask how you were doing. We still have people asking about both Don and Dorothea." Running the business in the 1980s and 1990s was very different than in the 2000s. Don speaks of the friendship that his community and business developed with the locals, a predominantly First Nations community. Until 2015, the inn gave credit to regulars for gas and food, and in the 1980s and 1990s, there was a music school in the Shepherd's Christian Society community and the inn hosted a weekly Friday night music-and-dinner event that ran for eleven years. The evening would start at five thirty and close down at a respectable nine o'clock at night.

"The first manager, his wife had a music school and they had a concert every night," Don says. "People would call to ask, 'Is the band playing tonight?'"

The inn didn't sell alcohol and didn't allow smoking in the restaurant.

"It was an illegal act [at that time], we didn't care," Don says. "One lady come in from Ontario with her daughter—when she found out she couldn't have a cigarette with her pie, she was ready to hang me. I comped her pie."

After the 1990s, the bus-tour and RV-caravan traffic slowed down, but the oil and gas industry boomed, and there was an increase in work crews travelling through the area. The recent downturn in the oil and gas industry is evident along the southern end of the Alaska Highway. From Dawson Creek to Buckinghorse River, lodges that became reliant on the industry have had a decline in business, and some have even closed completely.

The change in the inn's customer base is reflected in the decision to convert the dining room—which is no longer needed to accommodate large groups—into a C-store.

"We're still seeing some work crews, [but] 2016 is the slowest year we've had in a long time," says Ryan. "Business as a whole is down about 35 percent because of change in the oil and gas industry."

Don has a pragmatic way of looking at the unpredictability of a resource-based economy upon which the business has been partially dependant.

"Whenever it would go soft in the oil patch, we'd go down with it," he says. "We'd cut back on our expenses. If you're in business you have to be very aware of what's going on around you, so you can match it and try to stay either even or ahead of it, but don't get behind it, or down you go. It was pretty close some years." He speaks as if imparting an important lesson to his successor.

Over the last thirty years, the Shepherd's Inn has seen all kinds of travellers. In 2015 and 2016, there was an aged cyclist riding the length of the highway who has become a legend among the lodge owners.

"We had this one guy come through, he was riding his bike," Don says. "He was over eighty years old. He sat at this table, he could hardly get his face over his breakfast bowl, he was that bent over from riding. His son was supporting him and he was riding to Vancouver. He stopped here overnight. He was quite a gentleman."

Among the visitors is a whole subcategory of what Don calls "highway travellers in need."

"In the past we've had to help a lot of people out—give out free rooms," says Ryan. "In the last three weeks I've had about a dozen requests for free gas—people travelling the highway and running out of money."

Sometimes people take advantage of the hosts' generosity: one man asked Ryan to endorse a fraudulent cheque; a group of cyclists received a discount rate but then stole from the rooms. One time, a man's car broke down in the parking lot; he promised to get it fixed but abandoned it instead. Don and Ryan can rattle off an endless list of minor irritations that they appear to accept as part of the price of doing business.

During 2015 and 2016, the society renovated the front of the motel, and there are plans to upgrade the rooms. "If business picks up, we want to upgrade our fuel system—get a canopy," Ryan says. "Maybe start some more businesses for people in the community and go from there."

A close community of people are dependent on the long-term viability of the Shepherd's Inn, and the inn's ability to adapt to the fluctuations and changes in clientele has served the business well. But it's Don's attitude toward the relationship between the business and the customer that offers insight into why the inn has grown and survived since the early 1980s. "You gotta know the pulse of your business," he says, "in order for your customer to understand that pulse."

This page: Korey Ollenberger and Lory Dille bought Pink Mountain Campsite and RV Park in 2000. The couple met in the mid-1990s when Lory was working as a cook at Mile 175 Buckinghorse River Lodge.

Korey Ollenberger and Lory Dille also acquired Sikanni Chief (this page) in 2013. "[Pink Mountain] was really busy with the oil patch, the campers and everything," says Lory. "We needed more space, plus there's water wells [at Sikanni Chief] in the back, which benefited our trucking company."

MILE 175 BUCKINGHORSE RIVER LODGE

THE BUCKINGHORSE RIVER Bridge crosses over a narrow, whiskey-coloured body of water that travels west to east. Depending on the snowmelt, rainfall and time of year, it flows fast and high up the banks, or it's the opposite. On a mowed grassy rise north of the bridge, on the west side of the highway, there are four signs: *Bucking Horse River "Just Good Homestyle Food,"* reads one, and below it, *Buckinghorse River Lodge "Eat at the Buck"* and *Over 1,000 Truckers Can't Be Wrong*. To the right of an AFD cardlock sign, an automated fuelling depot that is accessed using a fuel card (like a credit card), is a *For Sale* notice.

Vel and Howard Shannon have owned Buckinghorse River Lodge since the mid-1970s. Howard (pictured at right) swears that the lodge is only as popular as it is due to his wife's cooking.

In 1999, Vel and Howard Shannon bought Mile 175 Buckinghorse River Lodge with Howard's brother, Lance, and his wife, Kim. Vel and Howard are now the sole proprietors. When they bought the lodge, it was in need of a lot of repairs. Although the Shannons have put a lot of time and money into renovations, Howard insists it's the menu that really put the lodge on the map. "The lodge is as well known as it is because of Vel's cooking," Howard says. "It's all her homemade recipes—that's why people come back." Over one thousand truckers can't be wrong.

The Shannons took a roundabout route to lodge ownership. They lived in Fruitvale, British Columbia, where they ran a restaurant, and Howard had a welding, fabrication and forestry-related business. "That's where I was born and raised, down there," Howard says. "When they did the NAFTA thing, it totalled my business."

The family moved to Fort St. John, where Howard got a job as a mechanical superintendent. Howard became frustrated by the lack of initiative at the company where he worked and took two weeks off to go hunting in the Buckinghorse area. Two months later, the Shannons were co-owners of a lodge. "I wasn't looking for anything at the time," Howard says. "It was a pretty good job, I was making eighty thousand a year. My dad thought I was absolutely out of my mind when we bought it."

"For Sale" signs are a common sight along the Alaska Highway.

Some people might say that Howard is a person comfortable with taking risks: in the 1970s, he was a drag racer, building and racing his own cars. "I probably spent the price of three homes doing that,"

Howard says. "I was an addicted drag racer—I spent almost all my waking hours doing that." This addiction led to temporary separation from Vel. Once Howard gave up the cars, the couple reconciled and have been together ever since.

The Shannons have two sons who live on the property with them. In fact, of the ten to twelve people who work and live there, only one is not a family member. "We have a cook, she's from Prince George. She's been with us for twelve years."

Howard describes Buckinghorse River Lodge as a seventeen-year reno project. The previous owners had the property for ten years, but it needed numerous upgrades. "The first thing we had to do was the water—two people couldn't have a shower at the same time, and the water was this colour," Howard says, pointing to the brown tabletop. "It's a well system—it wasn't treated or filtered or anything. Just raw water right out of the well." Then there was the electrical. "Whoever was here had no idea what the hell they were doing," Howard says.

The dining room at Buckinghorse River Lodge is an old US Army barrack.

"They never fixed any outlets, just ran one extension cord to another one—I took fifteen or sixteen extension cords out in the first month." Then the single-pane windows needed to be replaced. "When they built these old places they didn't worry about the cold, they just put more wood on the fire."

Opposite: Fire has been the death knell for many Alaska Highway lodges. Buckinghorse River Lodge has survived two generator fires since 2006 (as this soot-darkened out building demonstrates) and the cost of the fires has taken a financial toll on Vel and Howard Shannon.

The Shannons are conscientious about conserving energy and have considered solar and wind power, but installing the infrastructure is too costly. As at most lodges along the highway, the power is supplied by two diesel generators. These are kept securely in steel shipping containers with fire walls built in at either end. The Shannons have good reason to house their generators in a near fortress-like building. Since 1999, they've had two generator fires; the first was in 2005. "That cost us just about half a million dollars in equipment, supplies, generators, fuel tanks, lawn mowers, quads," Howard says. "There was a fifty-by-eighty-foot shop and I lost three generators." They had been storing building supplies for renovations and lost all of those. "Doors, toilets, windows, sinks. We've never really recovered from that." The second fire was in 2014, and that time the generator was brand new. Again, the family lost everything at a quarter-of-a-million-dollar cost. "The last fire I almost quit, but I just couldn't."

The Buckinghorse River Lodge's history begins decades before the Shannons' ownership (and generator troubles). The site of Buckinghorse River Lodge was a river crossing on the pack trail between Fort Nelson and Fort St. John, and in 1935, Wes Brown, a hunting-guide outfitter, and his family built a hunting lodge on the bank of the river. During the construction of the highway, the US Army used the site as a camp. The lodge at that time was on the east side of the highway, and to accommodate the fly-out hunting trips, an airstrip was built where the present-day parking lot now lies.

The lodge's years on the east side of the highway were the busiest time in the business's history. There was a restaurant, a liquor store, a gas station and rooms for rent. Wes moved what is now the lodge dining room, and an original US Army barracks with its coveted fir flooring, to the west side of the highway to use for his guiding business.

The Shannons have never guided any hunting trips out of their lodge, and they've had their busy and their slow times. As with many of their highway neighbours, the oil and gas industry contributed to the busy times. A camp was built on the east side of the highway in 2004, which operated for eleven years. "Everything slowed up here two years ago," Howard says. "It's been pretty quiet since. There's virtually no activity in the oil field–related stuff—basically the operator just looks after the infrastructure." The slowdown in the oil and gas sector is reflected in the Shannon's business, as they figure they are doing 40 percent less than they used to.

However, the decision to put the twenty-four-hectare (sixty-acre) property up for sale two years ago was not because of the slowdown in business but rather a completely unrelated event. In 2008, Vel and Howard were in a car accident in Prince George that left Vel with a broken back and five broken ribs. "Her internal organs aren't where they are supposed to be," Howard says. "She's getting to the point where she needs more medical attention." That attention is a two-and-a-half-hour drive south. Howard also admits that at sixty-eight years old, he's getting to the age where the work of maintaining the lodge is not as easy for him as it once was.

The Shannons keep their business open year round, which is easy for them since they live on the premises. "It's a lifestyle for us, too, basically," Howard says. "My wife says it's like camping out all the time."

The Shannons have played host to several celebrities, notably a grizzly bear who's graced the silver screen: Little Bart, the bear you may have seen in *Into the Wild*. (Little Bart is eight-foot-one-inch tall and should not be confused with Bart the Bear, who was nine foot six and appeared in *Legends of the Fall*. Both bears were trained by well-known Utah-based animal trainer Doug Seus.)

"They were filming in Alaska and were bringing him down." When the trailer transporting the bear pulled into Buckinghorse River Lodge, it was having trouble with the shower system to keep the animal cool. "They are out there spraying the trailer and I started giving him shit. Then I saw the bear and said, 'If he's hot then you'd better cool him down.'" The handler let Howard touch the bear. "He was massive— that bear stood about damn near five feet at the shoulders."

Once the Shannons sell the lodge, they'll hit the road. Their final destination will be southern British Columbia, where they have family, but first, they'll head north. The farthest north on the Alaska Highway that Vel and Howard have been is Mile 351 Steamboat. "We'll stop at Liard, and I've always wanted to go to Skagway and take the train," Howard says.

MILE 200 TRUTCH LODGE

YOU CAN'T SEE THE TRUTCH Mountain section—the highway now skirts around it—but it lives on in early highway stories as a sometimes impassable incline, and a treacherous decline. The remains of Mile 200 Trutch Lodge exist deep in the woods, a sketch of the business that—from 1950 to 1963—was run by Don and Alene

Peck. An old guidebook states the lodge was at Mile 201, whereas Ross Peck, son of Don and Alene, says it was at Mile 200. There was a highway maintenance camp at Mile 201, which is most likely what the guidebook was referring to.

Ross, who is a retired guide outfitter and a rancher living in Hudson's Hope, recalls that there were a few "Trutches" close to his parents' lodge: "Somewhere in there, another lodge came into existence

This is Schedule "A" referred to in the Bill of Sale made between Harry Noakes and Donald Ross Peck and dated the 4th day of January, A. D. 1.

ARTICLES listed in Service Station at mile 201, TRUTCH, B.C. Coffee Shop, Mile 201 TRUTCH, and BUILDINGS, EQUIPMENT, FURNISHINGS, etc., in CAMP 200½, Mile 200, and known as THE GOVERNOR GENERAL, owned by HARRY NOAKES, sold to DONALD ROSS PECK.

Chain Hoist
Tire equipment - irons, removers, spreader, etc.
Motor Rhythm - several cans
Instant Seal - " "
Valves, hotpatches - various sizes
Valve caps - various sizes
Jacks, large and small
Prestone - large and small cans for
Hydraulic Brake Fluid can with hose dispensing
Esso-Rad Anti-freeze
Alcohol Anti-freeze - several cans
Filterfill - several boxes
Sealed Beams - several boxes
Atlas Cement, etc.
Battery Straps
Hose Clamps
Oil Cans (four)
Blow Torch with soldering iron
Hot Patch machine
Transmission Grease Dispensers Two - One with guage
Large Pipe Wrench - Small Pipe Wrench
Fan Belts
Hand Grease Guns (Three)
Lincoln Grease Dispenser
Oil Measures (Two - 1 Gallon & 1 Quart - Imperial)
Can Openers (Two)
Funnels (Two)
Flourescent Lights (Two sets) NEW
Large Dispensing hose with fittings
Gas Pump hose with fittings
Nozzles for dispensing hoses
Water Pressure system (to be installed at Camp 200½)
Shelving
3 burner electric silex
Water barrol
Fire extinguishers assorted (several)
Work table kitchen, with upper shelf
Smaller table with drawer
All shelves in pantry and kitchen, 2 X 4's and wall board in pantry
Linoleum on kitchen floor
Diesel burning cook-stove (Quaker) & pipe, diesel tank connected
Electric Plate - 2 burner
Electric Toastmaster
Large Milk can
Water pails, mop & cleaning pail
Garbage pails
31 teaspoons   38 forks   48 knives
23 dessert spoons   5 enamel pie plates 1 rolling pin
1 fruit squeezer   1 spatula   1 meat fork
1 doughnut cutter   1 dish scraper   1 wire pastry mixe

This property inventory accompanied the bill of sale for Trutch Lodge, which Don and Alene Peck ran for thirteen years. The list includes everything from a chain hoist to hose clamps to a water barrel.
Photo courtesy of Ross Peck.

at Mile 195, which was also called Trutch and was run until it was displaced by the highway relocation."

Don Peck was a trapper, guide and packer who had worked with legendary surveyor Knox McCusker. As the Royal BC Museum's online Living Landscapes project explains, Knox McCusker was a lead in the logistics of constructing the Alaska Highway, but before that, he mapped out the Northwest Staging Route from Edmonton, Alberta, to Fairbanks, Alaska. The route was developed from 1940 to 1944 and was composed of airstrips that the United States used

during World War II to transport combat aircraft to their Russian allies. Alene was a teacher in Charlie Lake and Fort St. John, and she learned accounting and bookkeeping working for the Royal Canadian Air Force during World War II. According to Ross, his father wanted to use the lodge as a base for his outfitting business and also have the year-round income from offering services on the Alaska Highway.

Peck family lore tells that in 1949, Alene moved from Mile 47 Fort St. John, British Columbia, to become the first teacher in the new

There is barely a stick of timber left of Trutch Lodge, but during the time the Pecks ran the lodge there was a post office, restaurant, accommodation and garage, among other services.
Photos courtesy of Ross Peck.

school at Mile 1016 Haines Junction, Yukon Territory. At the end of the school year, in the spring of 1950, Don drove up the Alaska Highway and collected Alene, and on the return trip, the couple stopped in Whitehorse to get married. They arrived as newlyweds at Mile 200 Trutch Lodge, which they'd purchased from Harry Noakes. Mile 200 sat on the site of a former highway camp, and when the Pecks took it over, the property consisted of a café and a garage. You could say that taking over the business was their honeymoon.

"In later years, they acquired some additional land in the vicinity, including some agricultural land down by the Minkaker River," Ross says, "and an old gravel pit across the road."

Ross was born in 1951 and has three younger siblings: sisters Patty and Kathy and brother Timber. All the children, except Kathy, worked at the lodge, and Ross first started pumping gas at four or five years old.

"Somewhere in there I got the idea of washing car windows and hanging around for a tip—an early squeegee kid," Ross says. "That worked well until one day I tried it when it was a little too cold and left a layer of ice on a tourist's front window. He wasn't too pleased."

When the Peck family lived at Trutch Lodge, the local population included people from a Northwest Highway Maintenance Establishment camp, the lodges and a Canadian National Telegraph camp. There were enough children in the area to warrant building a school in 1956, which Ross attended from grades one through seven.

Don and Alene worked side by side at the lodge. "When a cook quit you could see my father in the café kitchen," Ross says, "and my mother would be out pumping gas when needed. Mother would cover in the café when needed—if the cook or waitress decided to run off with a truck driver."

Although Don had many bushcraft skills, he was not inclined toward automobiles, so Trutch had a mechanic among the staff. Alene used her bookkeeping experience to manage the finances. The business grew, and aside from the original café and garage, Trutch Lodge ended up with a store, post office, pool hall, motel, staff quarters, the Pecks' house and an airstrip. When their business was at its peak in the 1960s, they had about forty employees and the lodge was running twenty-four hours a day.

Don bought fur and traded with the First Nations people trapping and living in the area. Over time, his hunting-outfitting business flourished and he became a highly respected member of the outfitting and guiding community in northern British Columbia. According to Living Landscapes, in 1961, Don co-founded the Northern Guides Association and was its first president. In 1987, a mountain was named in his honour: Mount Peck in Tower of London Range of the Muskwa Ranges (in the Northern Rockies).

The Pecks ended up selling the lodge and became involved in other businesses. It appears that they learned that diversity in business was the key to success. Until Don passed away in 1980, the Pecks continued to run their outfitting and fur-buying-and-trading businesses, and had stores on the Halfway River and the Prophet River First Nations reserves. Don and his son Timber operated a stock-contracting business south of Fort St. John. Alene ran a store, Peck's Place, from her log cabin at Mile 49, where she sold moccasins and works by First Nations artisans. She now lives in a long-term care facility in Fort St. John.

What remains of Trutch Lodge today is a shadow of the former establishment. "Most of the buildings of any substance burnt down," Ross says. On a recent visit, he found "only one old shack on the property with trees going up through it and a few concrete foundations."

Opposite: The 1951 edition of *The Milepost* describes Lum 'n' Abner's as "a colorful and authentic north country trading post, with real log cabins having screen-porches, and equipped with beds having inner-spring mattresses." The lodge is now abandoned.

Left and above: You can piece together a fragmented history of the life of an abandoned lodge. It's easy to imagine work crews stopping for lunch in the café, or a frugal vacationing family choosing to fill up an extra jerry can because the fuel was cheaper than in Fort Nelson. Mile 351 Steamboat was burned down after these photos were taken.

MILE 375 TETSA RIVER LODGE

IF YOU'RE DRIVING ALONG the highway near Mile 375, don't be surprised if you suddenly smell cinnamon wafting into your car—it's not an olfactory illusion. It's very likely that Ben and Gail Andrews, who own and operate Mile 375 Tetsa River Lodge, are in the midst of baking their daily batch of cinnamon buns.

"I taught Gail how to do the buns, as this was an absolute necessity," says Ben, whose father, Clifford, and stepmother, Loryne, built the lodge in the mid-1970s.

In the early 1970s, Clifford and Loryne were leasing Mile 233 Prophet River Services when their business fell victim to the infamous realignment of the "monster" highway, which was the death knell of many lodges. As mentioned in the introduction, the highway has been shortened since it was first constructed through to Alaska. The original route was known for being a Godzilla of a road that, depending on its appetite, consumed entire vehicles whole in its seemingly endless number of curves, or merely snacked on tires and engine parts in its potholes. Slowly over the years, the more dangerous curves of the highway have been chopped out, leaving mind-numbingly straight sections of road that are interrupted by the occasional gentle curve.

Opposite and above: Tetsa River Lodge is a two-person operation. Ben and Gail Andrews run the café, gift shop, RV park and gas station by themselves.

"The highway bypassed them," Ben says. "Dad knew about Tetsa because he used to take geologists out there and knew it was for sale."

Tetsa had been the site of a construction camp in the early days of the highway, and when Clifford and Loryne bought the property in 1976, the only thing on it was an old building left behind from the highway construction.

"When they first moved here, they were just going to take hunters out," Ben says. "Winters were tough to make ends meet, and they started to squirt a little gas. Then Mom thought she might sell a few loaves of bread, and it evolved into what it is today."

Back in 2008, when Loryne and Clifford still operated Tetsa River Lodge, a visitor arriving on an overcast fall day could've mistaken the location for the set of a 1970s horror movie: a dark, forbidding and claustrophobic landscape; spindly and leafless trees; everything a little rundown; and the main building, a ranch-style log home where the reception area was crowded with taxidermy and covered in a thin layer of dust. There is a remarkable difference between how Testa looked in 2008 and the sheen it has in 2016.

Tetsa River Lodge has a gas pump but the real draw is the baking—the Andrewses somehow manage to find time in their busy lives to bake three hundred cinnamon buns each day.

"The place needed space and sprucing up in order to have room for product to sell," Ben says, "and the look that I think people think a lodge on the Alaska Highway should look like."

After Clifford died in 2009, Ben inherited the lodge and proceeded to clear trees and tidy up the lawn along the highway. Ben and Gail renovated the main building, and visitors can sit down in the charming restaurant for a cup of coffee and a legendary cinnamon bun that is slightly sticky and sweet yet tangy and chock full of nuts and raisins. Or visitors can browse books and souvenirs in the gift store. Tetsa may soon become as much renowned for the homemade sausage and bacon that Ben makes as it is for the cinnamon buns.

"I always made the bacon and sausage for us, and my Gail talked me into making it for the store," Ben says. "It has turned out to be a very good addition."

Ben and Gail have worked hard to bring the business around, and they put in long days, starting at four o'clock in the morning and ending well past eight o'clock at night. Their investment has paid off. Caravans of RVs have made Tetsa a regular stop for meals and coffee breaks. To satisfy their customer base, the couple bake an unfathomable number of cinnamon buns daily: three hundred. Ben and Gail are the only employees at Tetsa, and it's easy to understand how at the end of the summer they are exhausted from a season of eighteen-hour days, seven days a week.

When Ben was a child and his parents ran the campground and hunting-outfitting business, they'd hire the occasional helper.

"Usually just one with my mother, but then Dad would get some deadbeat to work in the yard with him, too," Ben says. "Sometimes he'd pay them, but it wouldn't be much."

Family labour was essential to the operations at Tetsa. For some years, Ben's grandfather Gordon Andrews was the resident mechanic. "He wouldn't rebuild a transmission, but minor things," Ben says. Ben is one of the six Andrews children, all of whom were recruited at some time or another to do tasks at Tetsa, including working on the construction of the main building.

"All the logs were skidded in by horse, peeled by hand, notched with an axe," Ben says. "I learnt how to build log homes and worked for a few companies building those in my thirties."

A childhood at Tetsa was busy: studying by correspondence, helping

Opposite: Summit Lake has survived through peaks and valleys of Alaska Highway traffic, and is now abandoned.

out with the business. Even recreation had to have a productive element to it.

"My dad said, 'If you want any time off here, you gotta go fishing.' I said, 'Why do I have to go fishing?' He'd say, ''Cause I like fish.'"

Being the only child for miles around had an effect on Ben. "It was pretty lonely," he says, "probably why I ran away at fifteen."

For Ben and Gail, their business is their lifestyle. They are open from spring to fall, and in winter they open when they feel like it. But by the turning of the leaves in September, the couple are pretty tired, and lately they have been considering their future plans. They have four children between them, none of whom want to take over the off-grid business.

Two generations of the Andrews family have operated Tetsa River Lodge, which was built in the mid-1970s by Clifford and Loryne Andrews.

"You have to be a unique kind of guy to be able to do that kind of stuff," Ben says. "We're not getting any younger. Why not enjoy life?"

Selling may be an option, but for now they are staying put. "We'd hate to sell it," Ben says, "but in some ways it's a real drain."

2. THROUGH THE MOUNTAINS, ACROSS STREAMS AND RIVERS WE GO

MILE 392 SUMMIT LAKE TO MILE 463 MUNCHO LAKE LODGE

Mile 392 Summit Lake Lodge **8**
Mile 397 Rocky Mountain Lodge **9**
Mile 408 MacDonald River Services **10**
Mile 422 Callison's / Toad River Lodge **11**
Mile 436.5 Double "G" Service **12**
Mile 442 The Village Lodge
Mile 462 Muncho Lake / Lakeview Lodge
Mile 462 Highland Glen Lodge /
    Northern Rockies Lodge
Mile 463 Muncho Lake Lodge

North of Fort Nelson, the area between Mile 392 and Mile 463, is arguably one of the most beautiful sections of the Alaska Highway. Running through the eastern Muskwa Range and the Battle of Britain Range of the Northern Rocky Mountains, and bracketed by two provincial parks—Stone Mountain and Muncho Lake—the entire area is protected as part of the Muskwa–Kechika Management Area. The mountains on both sides of the highway, the basalt outcrops that protrude from the mountainsides, the canyons and waterfalls, the unpredictable flow of rivers and creeks—this is a landscape that dares humans to inhabit it.

This section of the highway is the closest you'll come to driving the curves of the road as it was in 1948. Drivers have to go slowly, as the road rises and winds through mountains, then lowers and straightens out somewhat, across rivers and streams and along lakes. For added adventure, caribou or Stone sheep sometimes hoof across the pavement or linger on the soft shoulder, nibbling at gravel or leafy protrusions. If the weather chooses, as it has on occasion in the past, you could get marooned at a lodge as floodwater rushes down the mountains, along the beds of creeks and rivers, and washes out sections of the road.

Long before the Alaska Highway was pushed from Summit through to Muncho Lake and on to Liard Hot Springs, the Sekani, Slavey, Cree, Beaver and Kaska Dena First Nations travelled this corridor. The Muskwa–Kechika Management Area website refers to future plans to restore a traditional travel route—the Davie Trail—between two Kaska Dena communities in British Columbia: Kwadacha (also known as Fort Ware, or Ware) west of Fort Nelson and Lower Post near the Yukon border. By road, it's a 979-mile J-shaped journey between the two communities, but if you look at a map and imagine where the Davie Trail probably went, as the crow flies, the distance between the two communities is a third of that. The descendants of these First Nations sit on the Muskwa–Kechika Management Area advisory board and continue to live in communities along the highway corridor.

One Kaska Dena family in particular is noted for having made its home in the Toad River–Muncho Lake area. As Kaska Dena researcher Allison Tubman notes in her 2015 book chronicling the lives of her ancestors, *The McDonalds: The Lives & Legends of a Kaska Dena Family*, the McDonald family moved from the Yukon Territory in the mid-1800s—around the time that the Hudson's Bay Company

Opposite: Summit Lake Lodge has been closed for many years but the seafoam-green exterior walls remain a brilliant reminder of a past era. This photo was taken in 2011, by 2016 the glass was all broken.

established Toad River trading post in 1867. The company most likely moved into the area to take advantage of the trading opportunities with the First Nations people; however, the trading post was abandoned by 1890, and the descendants of the McDonalds remain in the area to this day. One of those descendants, Charlie McDonald, who died in 1975 at the age of eighty-one, is a celebrity among Alaska Highway construction aficionados. As Tubman states, Charlie was one of several men who guided the US Army through the bush to lay the roadway from Mile 351 Steamboat Mountain to Mile 620 Lower Post. Since the advent of highway lodge construction, the McDonalds often worked as either lodge staff or hunting guides.

Alaska Highway construction camps were located ten to fifteen miles apart and could accommodate a crew of up to two hundred workers. The Alaska Highway Heritage website describes a typical camp as having a "barracks, offices, one large kitchen and combined mess hall, a field shop, and a storage warehouse." After the highway construction crews left the camps and the maintenance and telecommunications crews took residence, lodges were built. It's easy to see how the old construction buildings would be turned into small communities at places such as Mile 392 Summit Lake and Mile 733.4 Swift River.

The 1950s were the blossoming years of the highway lodge community. The 1959 travel guide *Alaska Highway: Road to Yukon Adventure* lists nine lodges operating between Summit and Muncho Lakes; nowadays, this stretch of road has only four.

MILE 392 SUMMIT LAKE LODGE

ALONG THE ALASKA HIGHWAY, Frank Steele gained renown as a business partner of Clyde Wann, who himself was a pioneering businessman in the Yukon Territory. Clyde owned four lodges along

the highway and made his mark on Yukon aviation history in 1927 as one of the founders of the first commercial airline in the territory: Yukon Airways and Exploration Company.

Vintage signage takes on a sinister feeling at an abandoned lodge.

According to Gordon Steele, the fourth of Frank's six children, Clyde went to the North in search of the gold motherlode. After starting up the territory's first airline with his business partners, Clyde went into battle against his rival, White Pass and Yukon Route, in a no-winner aviation price war. "Clyde never shied away from a fight," says Gordon. "They both went broke."

Frank Steele and Clyde Wann became friends when they met in the 1940s in northwestern British Columbia, in Atlin, a village that was established after it experienced a gold rush in 1898. Like most gold rushes, the Atlin one didn't last long, but the area was mined for silver and gold for decades afterwards. It was a loan from Frank that gave Clyde the boost he needed to restart his business ventures in the Yukon.

"Clyde was always broke," says Gordon, who at seventy-nine years old lives in a tidy house in Riverdale, a suburb of Whitehorse, Yukon. "Even though he was probably a millionaire, he never had any money on him. The story is Frank lent Clyde twenty dollars so Clyde could get to Whitehorse, where he was successful in winning a contract to install telephone poles along the highway."

Clyde's business snowballed from that point onwards. In June

1948, Clyde married Helen Shaug in Coeur d'Alene, Idaho, and she would end up running the lodges with him. Clyde and Frank remained business partners until 1955, and the somewhat convoluted story of how Frank bought Mile 392 Summit Lake Lodge in 1957 involves his good friend Clyde.

"It's quite a strange story. Clyde owed my father money for back wages and turned over the ownership of 505 Steele Street in Whitehorse in payment," says Gordon. Although the Steele family lived in a house on a street bearing their last name, the street was named after the heroic Sergeant Sam Steele, who prevented starvation and chaos in Dawson City at the start of the Klondike gold rush by decreeing that anyone coming over the Chilkoot Trail had to bring their own supplies to get them through their journey and establish themselves in the goldfields, which became known as the infamous one ton of goods.

Then, in 1957, Frank used the Steele Street house as collateral to buy the Summit Lake Lodge from his bookkeeper, who was commissioned to sell it. The bookkeeper loaned Frank his commission from the sale of the lodge to help with the purchase.

Summit had been a highway construction and maintenance camp, and at certain times in its history there was a small community with a school and a post office. Frank ran Summit with his second wife, Del Frank, whom he met in Watson Lake while he was leasing Mile 635 Jac and Mac's Café.

Frank ran Summit Lake Lodge year round, twenty-four hours a day, from 1958 until 1976. "He knew it was time to quit when he became cranky," says Gordon. "To see all the lodges all close down was pretty heartbreaking for him. He saw them all start with the construction of the Alaska Highway."

After selling Summit Lake Lodge, Frank retired to Sardis, British Columbia, where he had a small farm. He later moved to Chilliwack, where he lived until he passed away at ninety-seven years old.

Summit Lake Lodge has been abandoned for many years now. Vandals and nature have been slowly eating away at the remaining structures, but its seafoam-green exterior walls—a colour choice Gordon says came after his father's time there—remain a brilliant reminder of what once was on the side of the highway.

"One of Dad's granddaughters on Del's side tells a story of a Boston Pizza commercial being filmed across the street from her hair salon in Chilliwack, when a man came in to get his hair cut. He said that he had once been a rookie cop up the Alaska Highway and that he was stationed in Fort Nelson. She asked if he'd ever been to the Summit, and he said that he would stop there almost every day for coffee. She told him her grandparents used to own the Summit. He said, 'You mean Frank?' He remembered the food and Frank's versatility. The man turned out to be Jim Treliving, chairman and owner of Boston Pizza International, the same Jim as on *Dragon's Den*."
—Gordon Steele

MILE 397 ROCKY MOUNTAIN LODGE

PEOPLE WHO REGULARLY DRIVE the highway near Summit Lake Provincial Park know that Mile 397 Rocky Mountain Lodge is just north of the park, but the question is, *Is it open?* For the owner, Chris Winkelmeyer, there is an easy answer: the lodge is open when he's there.

"It doesn't run all year round, only during the season," Chris says. "Depending on the snow, it could be April to September."

In some historical publications, the lodge is listed as Rocky Mountain Court or Lodge; in others, it's the Rocky Mountain Auto Court. The DeMasters built the lodge in 1953 and owned it until the 1980s.

"The DeMasters were open all year round, and they leased it out in 1975 to some Americans," Chris says. "They leased it for about six years—they did it only seasonally, summertime."

Chris purchased the lodge from the DeMasters estate in 1985. From 1985 to 1998, Chris was working in Fort Nelson for West Coast Industries and had staff running the lodge. "Sometimes two or one persons, depending on the business," he says.

The main building, which holds the restaurant and kitchen, was built in 1953, when the Alaska Highway ran on the west side of the lodge. The rock to the east side of the lodge was blasted away between 1953 and 1955, and the highway was rerouted to the other side. The two two-room motel units with garages were built in 1954 and 1955. Rocky Mountain Lodge was not the only lodge along the

Chris Winkelmeyer has operated two lodges in the Muncho Lake area. He and his former wife, Gail Stephan, ran The Village Lodge together, and later the Rocky Mountain Lodge.

The brightly coloured flag of Amsterdam flies at Rocky Mountain Lodge, which in the past was one of the few lodges along the Alaska Highway that offered garage storage for guests' vehicles. Nowadays, the lodge only offers fuel, snacks and a limited selection of items in the shop.

highway that offered garage parking. In the 1951 *Milepost*, Mile 1054 Silver Creek Lodge advertised garage facilities for guests' vehicles.

The lodge no longer offers the motel and garage rooms but sells fuel, a limited menu, snacks and "odds and ends." Chris, who's lived in the area for thirty years, spends his winters in warmer climates, such as Egypt or South America.

Chris and his ex-wife, Gail Stephan, previously owned The Village Lodge at Mile 442, and when they ran it, they offered accommodation, gas and guided tours. "We were only open in the summertime," he says. "We didn't offer boat tours, but I'd take a floatplane to different places to go hiking."

Chris's decision to operate Rocky Mountain Lodge is a choice made more for lifestyle than for profit. He is an avid hiker, and the mountains and open alpine landscape that surround the lodge beckon him.

"My favourite area would be Rock Pass, it's a couple of days to go in, a couple of days to go out. The geography is different, massive erosion pillars. You won't see it anywhere else," Chris says. "And you have glaciers there, which is very interesting. It's a wild area, so you have to know what you're doing. There are only game trails."

Over the years, Chris has developed a loyal customer base from Alaska and Yukon. Regulars stop in at the lodge for a cup of coffee, as well as baked goods and ice cream, both of which are homemade. "I know people from fifteen or twenty years ago," he says.

Land for sale in the area is nearly impossible to come by, except for Toad River and some parcels adjacent to Mile 436.5 Double "G" Service. Meanwhile, at Rocky Mountain, sandwiched between two provincial parks, Chris is adamant that his lodge is not for sale. One of his sons wants to take over the property, though not necessarily the business.

"Through the years you have experienced a lot of things here. I've seen Americans with Uzis driving through," he says. "In the earlier days, the RCMP would stop here more often, every couple of weeks, and it would be on a social basis—they would be more inclined to talk."

Like the majority of lodges along the highway, Rocky Mountain is off the grid; Chris runs the lodge on a generator and solar power. "Of course in Toad River they got electrical power, but that's only one place," he says. "If you don't want to be here and you want to make money forget about it. There are bigger places around that I could make money. I've travelled through the world and I've never seen anything like this."

MacDonald River Services has been closed for many years. Weather, vandals and curious souvenir hunters have had an effect on the business' remains.

MILE 422 CALLISON'S / TOAD RIVER LODGE

THE FIRST THING YOU NOTICE upon entering the Toad River Lodge restaurant is the hat collection that occupies every part of the ceiling and is creeping down the walls. The majority of the collection is composed of ballcaps, but camo-patterned US Army–issue canvas boonie hats with soft, wide brims are conspicuous among the stiff, curved bills of the ballcaps. Started by Bob Price in 1979, as of June 2016, the collection numbered just over ten thousand (and growing).

It may be simply a coincidence, or part of the job description, but many men named Bob have owned Toad River Lodge since it was first opened in the 1940s by some young people with dreams and

Opposite and below: Toad River Lodge is famous for its hat collection—which now numbers well over ten thousand.

energy to burn. But before the Bobs, there were the Callisons, and that means we have to go south down the highway back to Dawson Creek, where the Callison family story starts.

In 1912, Fred and Dora Callison made the one-thousand-mile-plus journey from North Dakota to the Pouce Coupe Prairie (now the Dawson Creek area) to take advantage of the bargain homesteading land price being offered by the Canadian government: ten dollars for 65 hectares (160 acres) of raw land. Then, Elisha (Lash) Callison was born on August 30, 1914.

The summer of Lash's birth was turbulent on the world stage. The SS *Komagata Maru*, with its 350 Indian passengers who had British citizenship, was refused entry into Canada at the Port of Vancouver, and Archduke Franz Ferdinand of Austria was assassinated, which precipitated the start of the Great War. Shortly after the war began, the tenant on the Callisons' ranch in North Dakota went off to fight. As Daisy Callison explains in her memoir, *Mountain Trails*, her grandparents Fred and Dora had to move their family back to North Dakota to take care of the ranch, and only in 1919 did the Callison family return to the Peace River region. About a decade later, the family moved north to homestead in Montney, north of Fort St. John. Lash, one of ten children, spent his youth trapping and farming.

The Peace River region continued to be remote until 1931, when trains starting rolling into Dawson Creek on the Northern Alberta Railway line. A year later, Winnie Parker from Hanna, Alberta, was visiting her uncle Ed Parker's homestead, which bordered the Callisons' property. She and Lash met, and four years later, they were married.

Shannon Soucie, who is a niece on Winnie's side of the family, has been working on a biography of her uncle Lash. She writes that Lash and Winnie opened a store in Old Fort Nelson, and then Lash spent some time working on the construction of the Alaska Highway, as well as a brief stint in the army at the end of World War II.

Opposite: Several men by the name of "Bob" have owned Toad River Lodge at one time or another. But the current owners, business partners Matthew Roy (pictured) and Darrel Stevens, have owned the lodge since the late 1980s.

Then the couple made their way to Toad River. Lash had first been in Toad River country in the 1930s, when he was prospecting. He then recognized the potential for a hunting-guiding business in an area teeming with caribou, sheep, goats, bear and moose, and without many people.

As the highway construction crews had finished their work and were moving out of their camps, Lash staked four hectares (ten acres) at Mile 422 and bought buildings left behind by the construction contractors. By then, Winnie and Lash had two sons, Gary (the eldest) and Grant. Lash built a house at Mile 301 so that Gary could go to school in Fort Nelson.

Lash's younger brother Dennis and his wife, Marjorie (Marj) Callison (née Clay), were married in 1944, and by the time they moved to Toad River in 1947, they had already operated the Rolla Hotel, in Rolla, British Columbia. Between them, the two couples planned to open a lodge, offer guided hunts, and farm and ranch.

The family establishment appears as "Callison's" in a 1947 list of highway services published by National Advertising System, Ltd., and it offered meals, lodging, gas and fishing. The Callison brothers started guiding that same fall. The accommodations and restaurant were probably basic, as the foursome were fresh into their new venture. As with many motels and lodges of the era, sleeping arrangements may have consisted of a cot or bunk bed, possibly in a shared room. There would've been an outhouse out back; hot water may have been a luxury produced on the cooking or wood stove. The lodge was off grid and ran on a generator—which, if it was a typical generator of the time, was often unreliable. In 1949, after about two years, the Callisons' business was fully operational and appeared as "Toad River Lodge" in the first issue of *The Milepost.*

The two Callison families ran their lodge and outfitting business together until 1953. Shannon Soucie writes that Lash and Winnie sold their part of Toad River Lodge to Dennis and Marj in 1953 and moved their house north up the highway—from Mile 301 to Mile 419—to start a ranch.

In 1966, Dennis and Marj sold the lodge to Bob and Maxine Kjos. The Kjoses had been hunting outfitters in Alberta, and after Bob flew into the Toad River area and took the bus south, he was convinced that this was the place where he and Maxine should move. And so began the first link in the chain of Bobs. Bob Kjos's memoir, *Horseshoe in My Hip Pocket: Lucky Again!*, recounts, among many stories, his and Maxine's lives as hunting outfitters and lodge owners, from the Alberta foothills all the way to Toad River. In the book, Bob recalls that when he and Maxine acquired the lodge, it had grown to include "a 14-unit motel, a café, a service station, staff buildings, saddle shed and barn on 200 acres—the hunting area was 90 miles long by 40–50 feet wide."

"We had no idea what we were getting into as far as the lodge," says Maxine. "Neither of us had a clue, but with a lot of help for the first couple of weeks from Dennis and Marj, we survived."

The schooling of children was a challenge shared among all the highway lodges. Some families tried correspondence classes, but most children had to be sent to other communities during the week or even for months at a time. Dennis and Marj Callison's two daughters, Gloria and Janice, went to school in Dawson Creek and lived with relatives there, as did their cousin Gary. By the time the Kjoses moved to Toad River and their children were school age, there was a school in Summit, a thirty-mile drive south down the highway. Later, a school was built at Mile 462 Muncho Lake, and then it was moved to Toad River.

"I learned more in those three years [running the lodge] than any other years in my life," says Maxine, "but I never missed the lodge for a minute. After we sold, we homesteaded six hundred acres of land just across the river from Toad. That is the place we love and miss, it will always be 'home' to Bob and I and our kids."

In 1969, the uncanny sequence of Bobs began: Bob and Maxine sold the lodge to Bob and Marj Fulton, who ran it for ten years. Then, in 1979, Bob and Donna Price bought the lodge. This Bob is the one who started the now-infamous hat collection. In 1991, Bob and Donna sold the lodge to Bob Clarke, who ran it for three years. Then Wanda and Rocky Southwick bought the lodge, putting an end to the rule of Bobs, and operated it for three years. Then, in April 1999, Matthew Roy and Darrel Stevens from Edson, Alberta, bought the lodge.

"We were in the logging business, and coal mining," says Matthew. "We basically were tired of the rat-race lifestyle stuff, and we travelled the highway the year before, looking for opportunities, and this is where we ended up."

The business partners and at-one-time brothers-in-law carried on the tradition of hanging hats from the ceiling, which has made the restaurant a unique attraction along the Alaska Highway.

"They leave the hats with the staff and we hang them up," Matthew says. "We try to keep them organized. We're always taking them down and washing them."

The main lodge building where the restaurant and gift shop are has looked basically the same since the 1990s.

When Matthew and his wife divorced, she moved to southern British Columbia with their two children, who at one time had gone to school in Toad River.

"My daughter came back and worked during the summers of her

university," Matthew says. "She waitressed, cooked—my son always helped outside." Darrel has two children as well, who both moved away from Toad River.

One of the oldest and longest-running lodges on the Alaska Highway, Toad River Lodge first appeared as Callison's in a list of highway lodges from 1947.

A mix of the old and the new, the lodge offers U-haul servicing and tire fixes and other minor repairs, plus the restaurant, RV sites and eighteen cabins.

"They had five RV sites when we bought the place, and that's the first thing we saw. We built that section up, we have twenty-three sites now," Matthew says. "Some of the cabins that are attached—they gotta be fifty years old."

Like the previous owners, Matthew and Darrel were drawn by the immense natural area surrounding Toad River. "I've always been an outdoorsy type of guy. I love hunting and fishing. One minute from your doorstep and you can be in the most pristine area."

The lodge is no longer at the mercy of temperamental generators: BC Hydro installed a diesel power station in the community in 2012. "The community had to build the power lines, the grid lines," Matthew says. "BC Hydro built the power station and then we sold the lines to them for one dollar. Before that we had our own generator. It was a big struggle."

The busiest season for the lodge is summer, when the owners hire nine employees; in the winter, they employ half as many. "We're open all year round, but we shut down for four or five days around Christmas," Matthew says. "Some days we wonder why we're open in the winter, but actually we do okay."

As is the case for other lodges, staffing is a challenge for Toad River Lodge. The business partners were able to find some staff through the Temporary Foreign Worker Program, a federal initiative through which employers can hire foreign workers after being unable to find Canadians to fill positions. Usually, though, Matthew says, employees come from Alberta.

"It seems like it's hard to get somebody from British Columbia because of the competition from the oil patch," he adds.

Although the work and business are nothing like what either Matthew or Darrel did before, they have no plans to go anywhere else.

"I ran heavy equipment, grew up on a farm, no service industry experience, and when I look back at it now... it's turned out fine," Matthew says. "We had people working at the start, but I've ended up working in the kitchen, lots just because you have to. People quit or whatever. I've flipped a lot of burgers and cleaned a lot of toilets, but it's turned out pretty good so far."

"The generator ran the lodge. Without it, nothing worked, no gas pumps, stoves, freezers and fridges, everything. One funny story: Dennis Callison was a great joker, loved to play tricks on people and have a great laugh. The first morning we were owners of Toad River Lodge, Dennis knocked on the door of the room we were staying in with, 'Wake up, Bob, your light-plant [generator] quit and needs to be fixed.' Of course he thought that was funny, and Bob had no idea where to start without Dennis's help. We had lots of light-plant problems, even with one as a backup, but finally in July of the first summer, they both quit and we were without them for three days. It was hell, we were super-busy, no cooling facilities [refrigeration for food], but we managed somehow and the new light-plant was bigger and of course ran better."—Maxine Kjos

MILE 436.5 DOUBLE "G" SERVICE

PANCAKES THE SIZE OF DINNER PLATES. Bread loaves risen to a height that defies normal leavening logic. These are the homemade treats that Jack Gunness bakes and cooks in the kitchen of the somewhat deceivingly plain facade of Mile 436.5 Double "G" Service. The squared seventh letter of the alphabet represents the two brothers, Jack (then thirty-three) and his younger brother, Charlie Gunness, who moved from Alberta to start their business in Muncho Lake.

"We were supposed to stay for two years," Jack says. "That was forty years ago."

The property was deeded to Burt Taylor, a mechanic in the US Army who worked on the construction of the highway. In 1969, Elmer and Betty Landmark purchased the lodge from Burt; the Gunness brothers bought it from the Landmarks in 1977.

When the brothers took over Mile 436.5, the property included a small store, a service station and a repair shop. After the store burned down in a fire started by the generator in 1983, the brothers built what is now the main building, which holds the café and storefront.

The combined Gunness families—Charlie was married, and Jack had seven children—ran the lodge together until 1981, when Charlie moved to Fort Nelson.

The allure of a promising resource economy drew the Gunness brothers to Muncho Lake. The region was close to growing oil and gas exploration. As well, there was the expectation that the Alcan gas pipeline would be built from Alaska all the way along the highway. Since 1974, the American and Canadian governments had been discussing having a pipeline linking Prudhoe Bay, Alaska, to the lower forty-eight through Canada. Different routes were proposed, but the Alcan pipeline plan was put forward by the Alcan Pipeline Company

Opposite: Double "G" Service relies on an old-school self-registration policy that is reminiscent of the days when truckers arriving in the middle of the night would cook their own meals in lodge kitchens and leave behind payment for food.

(which later became Alaska Northwest) in July 1976, and President Jimmy Carter became its champion in 1977. Ultimately, the pipeline proved too costly, and Alaska Northwest couldn't raise the capital needed. By 1982, the plan was ditched.

"We were going to make our fortune, this area was very, very busy," Jack says. "That era was at the end of the pipeline days, so the pipeline combined with the mystique of the tourism industry—we worked twenty-four hours a day, just go, go, go."

The four-room scribed-log motel was built in 1983, but since then, one of the rooms has been decommissioned. From the outside, the building has a similar worn look as the main building, but once you step inside the motel, the floors and walls are so clean, you can almost see your reflection in the wood.

After Charlie left the partnership, Jack started hiring outside help, though some of his children worked at the lodge.

Opposite: Although the dining area in Double "G" Service is small and seating is limited, the servings are enormous.

"One of my girls stayed with me for quite a while. She started when she was six, helping me baking," Jack says. "When she was fourteen, she was running the place when I had to go away."

Despite being a mere fifteen miles from the Toad River BC Hydro generator station, Jack can't access that community's power and has to run his business from his own generator, and this extra cost is reflected in the price of food, fuel and accommodation. "They would never run a line up here for me," he says. "It's always been that way, that it costs a lot to run on generators."

In the 1970s, Double "G" had three neighbouring lodges: J&H Wilderness, Muncho Lake Lodge and the Highland Glen. Of those three, only the latter is still operational but with significant upgrades and under a new name: Northern

Rockies Lodge. As Jack tells it, when there were more people living in the area, there was a greater sense of community and more facilities, including a school and a curling rink.

In his book *North to Alaska!*, Ken Coates describes the early curling rinks as "unheated, single-sheet Quonset huts." Time and again during our research for this book, lodge owners and community members mentioned the bonspiels, explaining how they'd travel miles to reach one. Coates writes, "The curling rink became a focus for social and recreational life in the long and often uneventful winter months."

Coates also gives credit to Walt Williscroft for the building of these rinks and the development of curling as the unofficial sport on the Canadian side of the highway. Walt began working on the highway

There's no shortage of coffee or colourful reading material for Double "G" Service customers.

in 1943 and was one of a group of men the Department of National Defence of Canada dubbed the "Original Group." These men were responsible for the design and construction of bridges and maintained the highway for eighteen years after it came under Canadian control in 1946. Walt became the superintendent of the northern area, and then held the same position for the southern area.

"We'd have weekend parties—we'd go to wherever the birthday person was on the weekend, or Saturday night," Jack says.

That old-time sense of good neighbourly relations extended to the travellers on the Alaska Highway, especially when travellers were in a jam created by Mother Nature. As you drive along the highway near Muncho Lake, you'll notice what look like rocky, wide dry creekbeds running perpendicular to the highway between the mountain peaks. These are the paths that snowmelt takes, and often in spring the water comes down fast, resulting in a flooded road. Over the course of his forty years in the area, Jack has seen the road flood about a dozen times. During these floods, it falls to the lodges to provide parking spots, food and shelter to travellers.

Double "G" Service offers welcoming accommodation for the road-weary traveller.

Jack also talks about the RV caravans that stop off on the way north or south. In the past, he's had to fulfill some unusual requests for the RV caravan tours that travel in groups of up to fifty or more vehicles.

"I'd have to order up a priest or a minister [for a service] from Fort Nelson," says Jack. "They come up for groups of one hundred or so, I'd never thought I'd be doing stuff like that."

Jack used to run Muncho Lake Tours from his lodge and would take people out on the lake in a boat. After the lodges on the other side of the highway closed, he no longer had access to the water. He also ran an RV park, and the posts signalling each campsite are still visible on the back part of the lot. His latest venture is subdividing the property. He has put ten lots on the market and is having some success with selling them.

The lodge is also home to the Muncho Lake post office, which has provided the only guaranteed income for Jack. In 2013, he received an award for thirty-five years of service from Canada Post. But the postal service is moving away from rural mail delivery, and once Jack "goes out, face-first on the grill," it will close the Muncho Lake branch.

Jack's seven children are scattered across Western Canada, from British Columbia to Saskatchewan. But Jack has no intention of leaving his home among the mountains.

"I'm going to die here," he says. "The kids don't want it. They grew up here, they don't want to live here, and I don't want to live anywhere else."

Opposite: Jack Gunness has no intention of leaving the place he's called home for the last forty years.

Mile 496 Lower Liard River Lodge 13
Mile 496.5 Liard Hotsprings Lodge 14
Mile 528 Dew Drop Inn / Chevron Inn
Mile 533 Coal River Lodge & RV 15
Mile 543 Fireside Inn 16
Mile 590 Contact Creek 17

After you leave the Muncho Lake region, the winding road begins to straighten out, and as you continue north through the Liard River corridor, the river snakes in and out of view. The region from Summit to Liard was once the Liard River Reserve and was divided into three provincial parks in 1957: Stone Mountain, Muncho Lake and Liard River Hot Springs.

Opposite: Colourful signage welcomes visitors to Contact Creek.

"Liard" is the French word for the poplar tree, and William C. Wonders (in his book *Alaska Highway Explorer: Place Names Along the Adventure Road*) suggests that Frenchmen who were working for the Hudson's Bay Company gave the river its modern-day name.

Tim and Marilyn O'Rourke ran the now-closed
Lower Liard River Lodge for many years. Their
year-round lodge offered lodging, groceries,
home cooking and even a heliport. The lodge
fell victim to vandals and was eventually razed.
This photo was taken in 2011.

This river was the first route into the Yukon Territory for fur traders working for the Hudson's Bay Company and geologists working for the Geological Survey of Canada. With canyons and rapids that have names such as Hell Gate, Devil's Rapids and Rapid of the Drowned, it's not surprising that travellers were keen to find an alternate route to the treacherous Liard, which they did: the Mackenzie River.

MILE 496.5 TRAPPER RAY'S LIARD HOTSPRINGS LODGE/LIARD HOTSPRINGS LODGE

DRIVING CHALLENGES ALONG the Alaska Highway are mostly limited to potholes, frost heaves and wildlife, notably the Nordquist wood bison herd that sprawls lazily across the highway near Liard River Hot Springs Provincial Park in British Columbia. But once upon a time, in the not-so-distant past, near Mile 496.5 there was a road sign that alerted drivers to the fur-spider crossing just south of the park. Ray Puttonen ("Trapper Ray"), the originator of the legend of the fur spider, was so convincing in his tall and broad tale—which told of an unusual insect crossed with a rodent—that park rangers had to actually deny the animal's existence to inquiring tourists.

"Ray was a really good storyteller—super engaging," says Brian Fidler, who worked at Mile 496.5 Trapper Ray's for five consecutive summers, from 1994 to 1998, when he was in his twenties. "He could even make it work while clipping his toenails."

While clipping his toenails? Brian explains that when he worked at the lodge, instead of building a curling rink or some kind of sporting venue, he and his co-workers started the "Penis Bone Players" theatre company. During one of the company's cabaret-style performances, Ray told a story as he clipped his toenails.

The questions continue to arise: *Penis Bone Players?*

Liard Hotsprings Lodge was once home to "Trapper" Ray Puttonen and his infamous bone collection.

Photo by Murray Lundberg.

"Trapper Ray was a collector of penis bones of all animals," Brian says. "He would stir people's coffee in the restaurant with one of his penis bones just to get a reaction."

Ray's "Trapper" moniker was not for his swagger or style of dress: he actively trapped in the area, and his trapline provided him with a supply of bones for his notorious collection, which he started because "they just looked pretty." Ray claims to have sold thousands of penis bones, and one made it as far as an art gallery in Germany.

"I'm the largest seller in the world at penis-bone earrings," he says. "Marten are offbeat sellers—for toothpicks or drumsticks for dolls."

The Penis Bone Players—who were gas jockeys, wait staff, cooks, mechanics and maintenance staff—lived in trailers set behind the lodge, in an area they called "the pit."

"We had these old-school trailers kind of in a circle and we built a stage with some logs and pulled up some earth," Brian says. "Trapper Ray packed it down with his front-end loader."

The theatre had a proscenium arch, a curtain and benches. Patrons could saunter up to the bar for refreshments.

"If there were any tourists passing through, and we thought they were interesting people, we'd invite them down to come and watch the show. It was basically like a big party."

"Trapper" Ray Puttonen was born in New Westminster and

moved around the province in a northwards direction before finding himself at Mile 496.5.

"It was an old lunch place called Wagon Wheel, run by a woman at Fireside," Ray says. He bought the property in 1986–87 with his then-wife, Jane Lansdell. The first thing they needed to do on the property was build a cabin to live in; then an RV park was put in, a tire shop was built and the main attraction, the lodge, was erected in 1990–91.

The lodge is perfectly situated on the opposite side of the highway from Liard River Hot Springs Provincial Park, where the campground is often booked up on summer days.

Ray and Jane ran the lodge together until the couple divorced. The Fort Nelson First Nation bought the lodge in 2000, and it has been opened and closed irregularly since then.

Brian fondly looks back at the summers he spent working at the Liard lodge in the nineties.

"I really loved being there, so many things came out of working there." While working at the lodge, Brian took a trip to Whitehorse where he met the woman who would become his wife, and the couple now have two children. Also, he has made a career in theatre: he runs the Ramshackle Theatre, which presents a cabaret-style performance on the couple's rural property outside of Whitehorse. "The work I do now," he says, "Theatre in the Bush, making theatre in the middle of nowhere, is what we did at Liard."

One legend claims that Trapper Ray died tragically and bravely in a battle with a bear on his trapline. The reality is that, after leaving the lodge, the teller of tall tales travelled south to spend time with his children. Then he retired, somewhat quietly, near Prince George.

As for his infamous penis-bone collection, it's fallen by the wayside. Although Ray is still a fan of the sword-like *os*, if one comes into his possession, he quickly moves it on to a new home. "I've got a wait-list," he says.

MILE 533 COAL RIVER LODGE & RV

Opposite: Generators are the hearts of Alaska Highway lodges—they run everything from fridges to furnaces. Brent Rogers is meticulous about the maintenance of the generators at Coal River Lodge & RV.

AS MENTIONED IN THE INTRODUCTION, Coal River is one of the oldest lodge locations on the highway. The original lodge was located on the northeast side of the highway. A fire in the 1960s destroyed everything except a small log cabin that was moved to the southwest side of the highway and absorbed into Coal River Lodge & RV, which is owned by Donna and Brent Rogers.

The Canadian government's 1948 guide to accommodation on the Alaska Highway explained that travellers arriving at Coal River Lodge could expect to purchase meals and gas and oil, have minor repairs done on their vehicles and sleep in one of fourteen beds. By the time the 1951 *Milepost* guide to the Alaska Highway was published, the lodge was owned by Mr. and Mrs. B.R. Kennedy (Mr. Kennedy was known by his nickname "Red"). It offered accommodation for up to thirty people, who could make long-distance calls if they wanted to, and the growing community of "trailerites" (drivers who were pulling travel trailers) could look forward to the electrical hookups that were to be installed at the lodge that summer.

The original Coal River Lodge was built in the late 1940s and Mile 533 is one of the oldest lodge sites still in operation.
Yukon Archives Rolf and Margaret Hougen fonds 2010/91, #1034. Photo by Rolf Hougen, 1946.

The Kennedys sold the lodge to Gil and Rose Skarat; then Gil's mother, Caroline (Carrie) and his stepfather, Lou Bagnall, bought the lodge. In *Reports from Hines Creek and Coal River*, Bill Hodson explains that in 1969, tragedy struck: a gas explosion in one of the cabins started the fire that destroyed the lodge. Carrie was in the cabin where the explosion occurred and was badly hurt. She later died from her injuries.

Adelle and Leonard Boettcher bought the property from Lou in 1970; they built most of the establishment on the southwest side of the highway, as it exists today. The current owners of Coal River Lodge & RV, Donna and Brent Rogers, sometimes offer that small original cabin as a low-budget and sparse accommodation.

There are two hubs at Coal River Lodge & RV. The first is the gas station and garage in the centre of the parking lot, where Brent can be found entertaining visitors and friends with jokes and stories. The other is on the far end of the parking lot, past the gas pumps and the garage: a tidy white building that hints at a past as a mobile home or office trailer. Here Donna runs the restaurant and kitchen. This is where you'll find home-cooked meals, shelves of her homemade

Opposite top: At Coal River Lodge & RV Donna Rogers bakes up typical homemade treats such as bumbleberry pie.

This small cabin is the last remaining building from the original Coal River Lodge, which was located on the opposite side of the highway.

Bison roam the landscape around Coal River Lodge & RV. If you're paying attention, you might see a bison "patty" or hoofprints in the dirt.

"Berry Delightful" preserves made from the berries picked near the lodge and a glass-front fridge full of apple and bumbleberry pies, Nanaimo bars and handmade berry-flavoured chocolates.

Out back, behind the garage and tucked neatly into a shed, is the roaring generator that powers the whole business.

The lodge had been vacant for a few years before the couple took it over in October 1999. In spring 2000, they opened their business. "It probably took us a couple of weeks to get it all tidied up and cleaned up," Donna says, "and we just opened it up just as soon as we could."

Before buying the lodge, Brent and Donna had lived in Fort St. John since the 1970s, and they were familiar with the area around Coal River.

"We'd come up, Brent and his buddies," Donna says. "It was in the late seventies, all through the eighties and nineties. Brent would sometimes come up once or twice a year, it would be late September, early October, to go hunting or boating."

The fifteen-hectare (thirty-six-acre) property includes a twelve-site RV park, six rooms in the motel and—a not-too-unusual facility for a lodge along the Alaska Highway—a landing strip.

Since owning the lodge, Brent and Donna have operated it seasonally from May to mid-September and employed three people each year. Two years ago, as the couple were approaching their sixties, they decided that it was time to put the business up for sale. As of fall 2016, the property had not sold.

"We are hoping that somebody with the same interests as we have will keep it going as a friendly place, clean and presentable and inviting," Donna says. "You can't make enough money here [in the summer] to get you through the rest because it's only five months. There's money to be made in the lodge--it's self-sufficient—but it's not going to get you through all year round."

The seasonality of the business has worked for Donna, for all these years. "I like the five months we're here," she says. "I enjoy it, and come September I'm ready to go home."

Still, the part-time operation of a large rural business has its challenges. One winter, the lodge was broken into: the windows had been smashed, and merchandise and other items stolen.

"It was a pain in the arse—what those kids were stealing... I'd left a couple of boxes of not expensive giftware—it had all my logo on it," says Donna. After that break-in, the Rogerses made sure to board up all the windows and doors, and empty the lodge completely. "We take everything out of here now. RCMP, truck drivers, friends go up and down the highway all the time and keep an eye on it for us."

This unofficial "neighbourhood watch program" evokes memories of yesteryear, when highway neighbours were concerned about each other's welfare along "the longest main street in North America." But it's easier to keep watch in an area that is not as isolated as Coal River. Farther north along the highway, the community is sparser and even more spread out.

Like many other lodges along the Alaska Highway, Fireside Inn has gone through a series of owners. The challenges of running a business that relies on vehicle traffic during a time when there is less and less of it have taken a toll, and at the time of publication, the lodge was for sale again.

This page: Richard Hair, pictured behind the counter, and his wife, Dennie, have run Contact Creek since the mid-1980s. Hailing from Florida, they enjoy their life running a gas station and coffee shop on the border of British Columbia and the Yukon territory. Craig Boettcher, seated, has a connection to highway lodges too—his parents ran Coal River Lodge for many years.

4. THE LONELY ROAD

MILE 596 IRON CREEK LODGE TO MILE 836.5 JOHNSON'S CROSSING

Mile 596 Iron Creek Lodge **18**
Mile 620 Christy's Lodge / Lower Post Lodge
Mile 635 Jac and Mac's Café
Mile 642.7 Upper Liard Hotel
Mile 687 Transport Café **19**
Mile 710 Rancheria Lodge **20**
Mile 721 Continental Divide Lodge
Mile 733.4 Swift River **21**
Mile 777.7 Morley River Lodge **22**
Mile 778 Welcome Inn
Mile 804 Teslin
Mile 813 Ten Mile Tavern
Mile 836.5 Johnson's Crossing Lodge **23**

Previous page:
Fireweed grows
through abandoned
tires near the remains
of Swift River Lodge.

Gold rushes of the late 1800s and early 1900s changed British Columbia, Yukon and Alaska. But the vague promise of an expansion of humanity and prosperity in the North from the influx of Klondike gold rush stampeders of 1897–98 to the Yukon Territory did not pan out. According to Government of Yukon statistics, Dawson City, the heart of the Klondike gold rush, which boasted a population of 40,000 in 1898, had a population of 2,038 in 2015. However, once the Alaska Highway was surveyed from Dawson Creek, British Columbia, to Delta

Junction, Alaska, there was no turning back. The Yukon Territory experienced a population increase as resource exploration and extraction became the backbone of the territory's economy. As if to salute the important role of the Alaska Highway in the future of the Yukon, in 1953, the territory's capital city was moved from Dawson City, on the banks of the Yukon River, 460 miles upriver to Whitehorse Mile 918 on the Alaska Highway.

At Mile 590 Contact Creek, the Alaska Highway dips northwards into the Yukon, still in the traditional territory of the Kaska Dena First Nation, and then swoops back southwest in British Columbia for another thirty-six miles before re-entering the Yukon five miles south of Watson Lake. Along this stretch of highway, you'll find rest stops and fishing spots. If you look at a topographic map of the Yukon, you'll see an intricately woven network of dirt roads lies across the landscape. If you're driving along the Alaska Highway and looking straight ahead, you won't notice the access points to these roads, which are at times just wide enough for an ATV. Blink-and-you-miss-it gaps in the tree-and-bush growth alongside the highway—these roads lead to prospecting camps, gold mines, fishing holes, bush-party fire pits, illegal garbage dumps and, at times, simply dead ends.

Remnants abound at old lodges, such as this forgotten spin caster at Contact Creek Lodge.

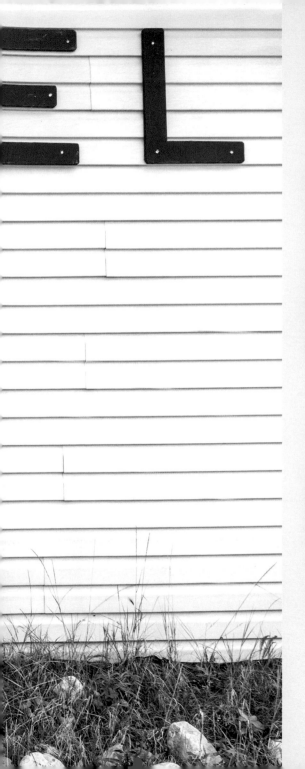

Iron Creek Lodge is one of the lodges that is for sale
along the Alaska Highway.

MILE 687 TRANSPORT CAFÉ

THE BRIDGE ACROSS Little Rancheria River is short, and if you're driving at regular highway speed, the dirt road on the west side of the bridge will flash past. But if you take that road and drive just a short way, you'll see the remains of Transport Café. The large café sign is stashed away in the bush to the west and firmly planted face-down. The old gas pumps have been removed, but their cement base remains, as does the foundation of the garage. Other cement foundations show where buildings once stood. The only complete building was dragged here sometime since the café closed. It's a pretty spot, if you can divert your gaze from the garbage that is beginning to accumulate. It's hard to imagine, but for seven years in the 1960s, the DesRosiers family made this place their home.

Netta (pictured) and John DesRosiers were the last owners of Transport Café. The couple ran the lodge for seven years before moving to Watson Lake so their children could go to school.

In 1960, the Yukon was an unlikely place for twenty-three-year-old Netta DesRosiers (née Zinck) to end up. Born and raised in Vancouver, Netta was building a career for herself as a chef in North Vancouver when she met her future husband, John DesRosiers.

"He stayed there [in Vancouver] for three years," Netta says. "Then we were married, and a month later he said, 'We're going to the Yukon.'" John had been working as an ironworker for Wright's Ropes, but his brother, Curly, and sister-in-law, Belle (née Dickson), of the long-established hunting-outfitting Dickson family, were operating an outfitting business in the Yukon Territory and needed help. So Netta and John packed up their automatic transmission AMC Rambler Ambassador station wagon and drove north. They reached their destination in what could be described as record time for any era: two and a half days.

Opposite: Poplar, lupine and fireweed overtake the former site of the Transport Café.

"We came out of Vancouver and slept at a friend's place in Ashcroft, and then we came from Ashcroft to Fort St. John, then Fort St. John to Whitehorse," Netta says. "We drove all day and half the

night, but we didn't get any flat tires, but we went into this pothole. Then after that I was going through so much transmission oil." The couple kept refilling the transmission oil until they arrived in Watson Lake, Yukon. "Not many people in those days knew about automatic transmission, but the junior mechanic in Watson figured it out—the return hose for the transmission got pushed off."

Their mechanical trials weren't finished, though, because the starter went at Squanga Lake. Luckily, a road maintenance crew was having dinner at a nearby café. "Afterwards these guys pushed us hard enough to jump-start the car. We didn't dare stop again until we got to Whitehorse."

John and Netta worked for John's brother, helping with the outfitting business for a few months. Then they moved to Whitehorse, and Netta worked as a cook and became the manager of the Taku Hotel restaurant on Main Street. "I got there at five in the morning—we opened at six—and didn't leave 'til five at night."

Netta DesRosiers has hung on to one of the coffee pots that helped her serve caffeine-deprived travellers in the 1960s—and it still works.

When Netta was twenty-eight, a tragic event propelled them to move out of town and take over Transport Café. "We lost our little boy. He was six months old. We lost him with crib-shadow death [sudden infant-death syndrome] and I just wanted to get away from there."

The couple didn't have much money, and a friend helped get them started.

"I had Alex Davis [a well-known hunting guide in the territory] co-sign for me with five hundred dollars, and we had to buy all the dishes and linen," Netta said. "It [the café] was locked up when we got there. The people who used to have it before, they shut her down. He was so mad at B/A Oil, he threw the keys in the river. We had to break into every room to open the doors."

On the Canadian and American sides of the Alaska Highway, fuel companies such as B/A Oil, which was taken over by Gulf Canada in 1969, opened lodges and either hired people or leased out the properties. Another arrangement was that an oil company installed fuel tanks and pumps in an existing lodge and charged the lodge owners a rental fee per gallon of fuel sold. The DesRosierses bought Transport Café from B/A Oil with no money down, and had to pay the company three cents on the gallon until they paid the debt in full.

"We were top sales of B/A or Gulf for five years for the whole Yukon," Netta says.

John and Netta had visions of running the lodge on their own—their remote paradise by the river. But the demand of truckers wanting twenty-four-hour service soon destroyed the dream. They had up to four people at a time working for them, though in the winter it was just the two of them.

After years of being abandoned, the Transport Café property is slowly becoming a hunting camp / bush-party site / dumping ground.

Transport companies were important customers for lodges, and they went through a lot of tires. So many, in fact, that the companies had tires in reserve at several lodges, such as Transport Café. "Each trucking company left their own tires there so it would be on its own trucks, it would be chalked with the trucking name," Netta says. "They didn't do it at all the lodges. We had stock for quite a few because we were open all night."

When John and Netta arrived, Transport Café consisted of three trailers, one of which was elaborately decorated by an unknown artist. "It had a picture of the Alaska Highway painted on it at the end of the building, and there was the picture of the five-dollar bill with Otter Falls painted on it, too." After they left the lodge, the "painted" trailer was transported to Dease Lake.

John did the maintenance and mechanical work, and Netta ran the accommodation and restaurant. Her secret to feeding highway travellers was a limited menu.

"I usually always had stew, roast or roast turkey, and I had different sandwiches," she says. "I only kept two different meals on the menu, or an omelette, so you can keep it fresh. If you had a big list of stuff, you're bound to have it go bad."

Coffee was a mainstay, which she made with the Corelle Corning-Ware coffee percolator she received for a wedding present.

"It's still working," she says. "I ran Transport on two of them, all those years. We always had fresh coffee. It only makes ten or twelve cups, so as soon as one got anywhere near empty, I got the other one going."

While living at Mile 687, the couple had two daughters. Their eldest, Karla, found life at the lodge lonely, and she longed for playmates. She had an imaginary family and siblings, but one day she was "nearly stolen" while playing with a carload of children whose mother had stopped at the lodge.

"I was busy cooking and waitressing, cleaning the tables off, taking the dishes into the kitchen," Netta says. "I looked up and I saw this woman pushing Karla into the back of her car."

Netta ran as fast as she could to catch up to the car. She banged on the driver's door. The woman stopped her car and rolled down her window. She asked, "What do you want?"

"I says, 'You pushed my daughter into your car.' She looks in the back. She just about started crying. She says, 'I didn't do it on purpose. You can see by the amount of children I've got that I wouldn't need any more.' She was really upset—she'd accidentally just pushed one more in the car. And of course Karla wasn't going to say anything—she had all these kids to play with."

At the age of three, Karla finally got her wish for a younger sibling when her sister, Dalyce, was born. John and Netta's decision to move from the lodge happened after Karla spent her first year going to school in Watson Lake, fifty-two miles east.

"She had to board away for her first year of schooling," Netta says. "Her dad would come and get her every weekend. After Karla was boarding away for school, I said to John that we weren't going to do that anymore."

The family moved to Watson Lake, where they bought a sawmill. They rented out the lodge to Cliff Ellis, who ran it with a business partner for about two years. Netta returned for one summer afterwards to run the lodge—to provide accommodation and meals to a government work crew—but then they closed the business forever.

During the seven years that John and Netta DesRosiers ran the lodge, they had generator problems, staffing issues ("If the waitress was pretty, the truckers took her," Netta says) and three fires, and they worked endless hours. But they also made many friends and memories they cherished for years after leaving Transport Café.

John passed away in 2014, and Netta continues to live in Watson Lake. The town is also home to two of her children: Dalyce and son

Lorn (the fourth born). The infamously social Karla is a well-known real estate agent in Whitehorse.

Every once in a while, Netta has someone drive her out to Transport Café. "It's part of my life, but wild horses couldn't drag me back to another one, 'cause you had no time to yourself."

MILE 710 RANCHERIA LODGE

Rancheria Lodge was the first lodge built between Watson Lake and Whitehorse by the British Yukon Navigation Company, a subsidiary of the White Pass and Yukon Route, which had a monopoly on river and rail travel corridors into the Yukon.
Yukon Archives, Rolf and Margaret Hougen fonds, 2010/91, #1038. Photo by Rolf Hougen, 1946.

THE BRITISH YUKON NAVIGATION Company (BYNC) ran buses between Dawson Creek and Whitehorse (later extending service to Scotty Creek, Alaska), and built the first lodge between Watson Lake and Whitehorse Mile 710 Rancheria Lodge, which opened on October 9, 1946. BYNC also built lodges at Koidern and Dry Creek, both now closed.

William ("Bud") Simpson helped build Rancheria, and when the people who were supposed to manage the lodge backed out, he and his wife, Doris (née Callison), put a down payment on the lodge and started to run it. The Simpson family first lived in what Gay Frocklage, the middle child of the five Simpson children, calls "a shack" on the property. When the lodge was constructed, it was a simple log building, and until 1976, the Simpsons added a beer parlour, a cocktail lounge and motel rooms.

Bud Simpson was born and raised in Telegraph Creek, British Columbia. His grandfather had been an agent with the Hudson's Bay Company and settled in the area.

"Ninety-nine percent of people knew him as Bud," says Gay.

Gay's parents met at the remote Simpson family homestead in Telegraph Creek. Doris was the second-oldest daughter of the Callison's ten-child-strong brood. (Her brothers Lash and Dennis and sisters-in-law Winnie and Marj would later build and operate Mile

422 Toad River Lodge.) In 1936, Fred Callison—the forty-nine year-old patriarch of the Callison clan—led a fifty-eight-day cross-country prospecting trip on horseback through British Columbia from Fort St. John to McDame Creek, then to Dease Lake, and finally to Telegraph Creek. On this journey were four of his children: John, Doris, Daisy and Dennis. When they reached their destination, Doris stayed at the Simpson homestead, where she met Bud. A year later, they were married in Vancouver. Daisy recounts the expedition experience in her memoir, *Mountain Trails*.

Linda and Denis Bouchard take pride in running a clean and welcoming lodge. They have infused their property with personal touches such as the "Elvis Wall" in the lounge.

The first owners and managers of Rancheria Lodge were Bud and Doris Simpson. Two of Doris's brothers and their wives opened Toad River Lodge in 1947.

At Rancheria, Bud and Doris ran the lodge as a team. They divided the work along traditional roles, with Bud managing the tire shop, anything mechanical and the cocktail lounge. But if they were short-staffed, Bud would be washing dishes or doing laundry. Doris ran the kitchen, but she'd take her turn at the gas pumps and beer parlour too. The Simpson children worked at the lodge, and they were always paid for whatever they did.

"You still had your family chores to do, but if you put in a shift in the restaurant, you were paid a full shift just like any other waitress would get paid," Gay says, from her home now in Dease Lake, British Columbia. "I think it was about a hundred and twenty dollars per month when you worked seven days a week."

As was the case for most families living in remote locations along the highway, for the Simpsons, their children's education proved to be a major challenge. There were three girls and two boys, and the choices for schools were limited.

"Me and my older brothers did grade one by correspondence. Grade two to grade twelve was in different locations and different dorms," Gay says. "All highway kids did that—I went to school in Swift River and Whitehorse in the Yukon, Duncan in British Columbia, and I graduated from Camrose Lutheran College in Alberta."

Gay describes going away to school as the worst part of growing up in a lodge. "That was devastating for everybody. We only came home at Christmas, and we'd leave in September, and we wouldn't be back again until June." She estimates that between grades two and twelve, she was home with her parents for about one year in total.

Among other improvements to the original lodge, Bud and Doris Simpson added a beer parlour, motel rooms and RV sites.

"When the fires came through in July 1958, they just about wiped out the whole area of the road there. There was no such thing as evacuations in those days. You just stood and fought, or you ran like hell on your own. I went to work at five thirty in the morning and looked out the window of the restaurant. It looked like a bomb went off up the valley at 718. Then it was on the move. By midafternoon it was at Rancheria 710, then it went from 718 all the way to Transport Café area. My parents packed everything they wanted. Everybody jumped in the vehicles. My dad and a few men stayed back and fought it and saved it [Rancheria Lodge]. No one was injured. When we came back the next morning, they were all staggering around, covered in soot, and the buildings were all sooted up. There was a lot of smoke damage. Some of the trees right in the yard burnt, but the men saved every building. There was some effort put in by the menfolk."—Gay Frocklage (née Simpson)

Like the DesRosierses at Transport Café, during the late 1960s, the Simpsons kept their lodge open twenty-four hours a day, seven days a week and all year round. The relentless workload took a toll on Bud and Doris. They only had their first holiday away from Rancheria in 1958, twelve years after they'd first opened the lodge.

"You just get more than your fill of tourists," Gay says. "You get ten good ones and one pain in the ass, and the pain in the ass ruins your whole day."

Gay knows about working in the tourism industry. She and her husband ran Forty-Mile Flats truck stop on the Cassiar Highway in British Columbia for twenty years.

Bud and Doris did try to move out of running the lodge in 1967. "They had other people running it, [but] they ended up burning down the main building," Gay says. The large motel was lost in the fire in 1969; it included an apartment that Bud and Doris kept on the property.

"It was devastating for them 'cause they thought these people were going to be successful," Gay says. "Mom and Dad had to go back, start at square one and build it all back up."

Finally, in 1976, after running Rancheria for thirty years, the Simpsons sold it to a woman named Beverly Dinning, who owned it for thirty years. Current owners Linda and Denis Bouchard bought the lodge in 2006, when they were in their late fifties. The couple moved from Horsefly, British Columbia (a town smaller on a map than the insect that is its namesake).

At Rancheria, Linda serves as many homemade menu items as she can to the truckers, tourists, locals, construction crews and the US military personnel moving between Alaska and the lower forty-eight. "Hamburgers, pierogies, cabbage rolls, tarts, cookies," Linda says. "I don't have time for bread or cinnamon buns. All our specials are homemade."

The occasional act of nature reminds people of the importance of a lodge oasis in the middle of nowhere. In June 2012, flooding, mudslides and rockslides closed the Alaska Highway at several points. West of Rancheria, Canyon Creek completely washed out the highway, and with mudslides blocking the highway to the east of the lodge, about a hundred people were stranded for four days at Rancheria. Food and water were limited, but Linda, Denis and their staff managed to provide essential services under the unexpected deluge of customers. The road wipeouts made national news, with *The Globe and Mail* running an article on June 11 titled "Food Scarce in Yukon Towns Cut Off by Flooding." It described the effect of the Alaska Highway shutdown on produce departments in Whitehorse's grocery stores: only radishes and coconuts were for sale. Tim Hortons opted to fly in 4,850 pounds of coffee and doughnuts to its two Whitehorse locations. Eventually, a single-lane, gravel pioneer road was built over the creek, and travellers, as well as food and fuel delivery trucks, could move on.

At Rancheria Lodge, the Alaska Highway tradition of home-cooked meals continues with both Denis and Linda taking turns in the kitchen.

But the future is uncertain for Rancheria Lodge. Linda was diagnosed with lung cancer early in 2015, and although she is feeling good after successfully finishing chemotherapy in June 2016, the Bouchards have been considering their next step.

"Nobody's buying lodges anymore," Linda said in 2015. "We love it, but we're burning out. We've had one holiday since we've been here."

MILE 733.4 SWIFT RIVER LODGE

FROM THE 1940s TO THE 1960s, a small community existed in the vicinity of the Swift River Lodge, which was owned by Clyde Wann (who held three other lodges) but was managed by Frank and Evelyn Steele from 1947 to 1954.

On the opposite side of the highway from the lodge was a camp where Canadian Northern Telecommunications repeater station and highway maintenance staff and their families lived. There were enough children in the area to warrant a school that went from grade one to five. There may have been a highway separating the lodge from the camp, but the children and adults moved fluidly back and forth across the roadway.

"We were fishing, there were kids all over," says Gordon Steele, son of Evelyn and Frank. Gordon was born in 1946 and spent seven years of his childhood with his siblings at Swift River. "The [highway] surveyors at that time used horses, so we'd steal their horses. It was a great place to grow up."

Frank Steele's family had been farmers in Saskatchewan and moved west to Ladner, British Columbia, after the drought of the 1930s. It was there where Frank met his first wife, Evelyn McPhadyen. Many families, such as the Steeles, the Campions, the Talbots, the Couches and the Suffesicks, lived at Swift River, and they

Gordon Steele (wearing a Yukon tartan–patterned tie) is Frank and Evelyn Steele's youngest son. He spent his childhood at Swift River Lodge, which his parents managed for Clyde Wann.

developed lifelong connections. Helen and Orvil Couch became Gordon's godparents.

The unique military history of the region meant that the Steeles sometimes had planes pull up to the fuel tanks for a fill-up. Before the highway was built, there was a series of landing strips from Edmonton to Fairbanks as part of the Northwest Staging Route. The US Air Force used these airstrips to transport planes to Fairbanks and onwards to the Russian allies. Many of the pilots were members of the Women Airforce Service Pilots (WASP), the first women to serve as pilots in the US Air Force. Small aircraft traffic along the highway route is still common today. At Swift River, the highway was used as an airstrip, and it wasn't that unusual for aircraft to make a stop for

Clyde and Helen Wann owned four lodges along the Alaska Highway: Swift River (opposite and below), Morley River, Destruction Bay and Beaver Creek. When a customer arrived the staff was tasked with promoting the other Wann lodges. Swift River was torn down in the summer of 2016.

services. "A plane would fly over, we'd stop the traffic, they'd pull up to our pumps and we'd fill it up," says Gordon.

The Steele family moved to Whitehorse in 1954 so that their children could attend the higher grades of school, but Frank never liked the city. He continued his partnership with Clyde and ran Clyde Wann Motors and Circle Service for one year. Then his marriage with Evelyn came to an end, and Frank moved to Watson Lake to lease Jac and Mac's Café.

During the time that Clyde Wann ran Morley River Lodge, Gordon was too young to work in the lodges, but when his older brothers, Cliff and Don, were teenagers they went to work at Morley River, forty-four miles west of Swift River.

"They were supposed to hand out a card with every fill-up [that read] 'Thank you for stopping at Clyde Wann Services and here's the next Clyde Wann lodge on the road,'" Gordon says. His brothers were independent-minded teenagers, and when they were busy at the gas pumps, they simply didn't give the cards to the customers. "Clyde says, 'Well you've got to hand out these promotional cards whenever you fill somebody up.'"

When Don refused to hand out the cards, Clyde fired him and told Cliff to take his brother's place. The two brothers were very loyal to each other, and Cliff could not abide seeing Don lose his job. The end result was that both boys lost their jobs, but they still hung around the lodge for close to a week while waiting for a bus ride home. "Clyde was stingy and wasn't going to feed them. The cook was sneaking them food. When Clyde's wife, Helen, found out that her husband was maltreating the Steele boys, well, Clyde was in the doghouse," says Gordon.

Swift River Lodge passed from one proprietor to another. The final owners were a pair of siblings who ran the lodge for sixteen years, but they ended up having to abandon their business when they couldn't afford to make the costly septic upgrades required by the territorial government. Since then, nature has been slowly over-taking the site. The aspen seedlings have sprouted through gravel, soapberry bushes are spreading their spindly branches, and the rigours of the seasons, rainfall, snow accumulation and icemelt are wearing down the exterior.

Opposite: Cellular phone service is still intermittent along the Alaska Highway but functional phone booths are becoming scarce.

Clyde Wann was notoriously stingy with coffee beans and portions at his restaurants. "There's a story of a tourist stopping at Morley River and wanting to spend the night there, and he said to Clyde, 'As soon as I smell your coffee boiling I'll be up.' The truckers sitting at the counter said, 'Sir, if you can smell Clyde's coffee, you've got a pretty good nose.' Once, a waitress was serving and took out breakfast, and Clyde sees the plates, and says, 'That's too much,' and takes bacon off the plate."—Gordon Steele

Morley River Lodge was the second lodge owned by Clyde and Helen Wann that a traveller driving north on the Alaska Highway would encounter.

MILE 836.5 JOHNSON'S CROSSING LODGE

REMEMBER OUR "HITCHHIKER" Gertrude Baskine from Toronto? When she arrived at Johnson's Crossing in the summer of 1943, the construction camp was a hub of activity. In the dispatcher's office, Gertrude was "proudly told that this camp would some day be the site of a new town. I quite believe it."

Things didn't turn out as predicted.

Robert (Bob) and Elly Porsild had led an adventuresome life in various remote parts of the Yukon with their young family before moving into Johnson's Crossing and starting a two-generation tradition of running the lodge. For four years, starting in 1929, Bob helped his brother Erling drive reindeer from Alaska to the Eastern Arctic to start a Canadian government reindeer farming industry initiative, a story Wendy Dathan recounts in her book *The Reindeer Botanist*.

Bob and Elly went into gold mining with some partners at Sixtymile on the Yukon River. In spring of 1946, the Jacquot brothers of Burwash Landing hired Bob to build the Kluane Inn. Then, in the summer of 1947, after the army vacated Johnson's Crossing, Bob and Elly settled their family on the land bordered by the Teslin River and the Alaska Highway; Bob had the contract to take down the former construction-camp buildings.

There was a fair amount of work to be done on the property: the mess hall and repeater station had to be demolished. Bob could do what he wanted with the remaining Butler huts (Quonset-style buildings) and sheds.

The Porsilds weren't young entrepreneurs when they started up Porsild's Café in the fall of 1947: Bob was just shy of his forty-ninth birthday and Elly was forty-four. They had four children (three girls and one boy), but that didn't stop them from starting construction of the lodge in early 1948. The lodge opened on April 7, 1949, although

as Ellen Davignon (one of the daughters) recalls in her memoir, *The Cinnamon Mine: An Alaska Highway Childhood*, "the term 'tourist lodge' might have been just a tad grandiloquent." There was no hot or running water, limited and immediate heat was provided by a barrel stove, the furniture matched in a liquorice allsorts kind of way, but guests were treated to Elly's piano playing and Bob's many stories of adventure.

"When the lodge was built, Dad wanted to call it 'Big Trout Lodge,'" says Ellen Davignon. Her father went as far as making matchbooks to promote the lodge under its new name. "On the back, there was a drawing of a man in a kilt saying, 'Will Ye No Come Back.'"

"It was weird," says Aksel, Ellen's older brother.

"My dad was Danish," Ellen explains. "There wasn't a Scot's blood in him."

"Except in spirit," Aksel adds.

When Ellen and Aksel are in a room together, the siblings, who are two years apart, tell stories in a weaving way: Ellen begins, Aksel intervenes with a new bit of information from another angle, Ellen overlaps with more detail and Aksel finishes with a flourish.

Every member of the Porsild family except Bob hated the name Big Trout Lodge, and after some discussion, the lodge was labelled "Johnson's Crossing" with finality.

Opposite: Bob and Elly Porsild opened Johnson's Crossing Lodge April 7, 1949. The lodge remained in the family through two generations of Porsilds.

Bob and Elly Porsild did hire some help from time to time, but they mostly did the work themselves.

"My mom was really hard to work for because she was so exacting—she wanted everything done exactly so, especially after we had the lodge," Ellen says. "I remember more than one girl pitching that broom and mop at Mom and saying, 'You want this floor clean, mop it yourself.'"

The kids helped out too. They began working at the lodge from the moment the café doors opened. Aksel remembers washing dishes, but he also helped with the fishing charter business. Because at the time, true to the Scottish-inspired name Bob had wanted, many fish (including trout) swam in Teslin River and Teslin Lake.

"We took parties out for fishing. We had a couple of sixteen-foot boats, and that was more or less my job," says Aksel. "Then I got a boat and motor of my own and I was able to keep all the money."

Aksel took guests out for two hours at the most, and if they didn't catch fish, they weren't charged. "There wasn't much limits for fish," Aksel says, "so they'd catch as much as they wanted."

Aksel says there were so many grayling in the river at the time, visiting fishers could catch up to fifty in one hour.

Elly stopped illegally serving wild sport fish to her customers the day she brought out her menu to a conservation officer. He informed her that she could not serve grayling in her restaurant.

"Yes, I can," she replied. "I sell lots of grayling."

The fishing charter price was a mere three dollars per hour, plus fifty to sixty cents for a gallon of fuel. The money Aksel earned went in part to his smoking habit, and cigarettes also happened to be inexpensive: twenty-five cents a pack.

"The kids smoked cigarettes," says Ellen. The source of the cigarettes would raise modern-day eyebrows: their parents. "Aksel got a carton of cigarettes for his thirteenth birthday and a box of soda crackers and a pound of butter. We were pretty far from stores, so you had to be imaginative. Nowadays that would be tantamount to child abuse."

"It set me off on a life of decadence," Aksel says. "I smoked for thirty-five years." He did eventually quit in 1988 and hasn't smoked since.

"I never learned how to inhale," Ellen says. "I really wanted to."

"Everybody smoked," Aksel says. "You went to someone's house and there was a box of cigarettes on the table."

To hear Ellen and Aksel tell it, the Porsild children lived a normal, untethered Alaska Highway childhood. But unlike at many other lodges, the children didn't have to travel far to go to elementary school; in fact, it was a mere six miles from the lodge to the school at Brook's Brook, just east down the highway. However, for high school, they went to Whitehorse, but Aksel also spent one year of high school in Dawson Creek.

Siblings Aksel Porsild and Ellen Davignon grew up helping their parents run the Johnson's Crossing Lodge. Here the pair sit in Ellen's living room on the bench of the family piano their mother Elly played to entertain family and lodge guests.

After graduation, Aksel didn't stray far from home. He was hired to drive gravel trucks for the Northwest Highway System, and he lived at the Brook's Brook highway maintenance camp for a while.

"I mostly stayed in the central section, from Whitehorse to Liard River," Aksel says. "I was in Swift River, Coal River and Liard River."

Johnson's Crossing is situated near the confluence of Teslin Lake and Teslin River, a very excellent spot for fishing for trout and grayling.
Yukon Archives, Rolf and Margaret Hougen fonds, 2010/91, #1043. Photo by Rolf Hougen, 1946.

After Ellen finished high school, when she was eighteen years old, she married Phil Davignon.

"One of the conditions of us getting married was Phil had to run the tire shop at the lodge," she says.

Adding their new son-in-law to the employee roster was a very practical solution to hiring help for the Porsilds.

Ellen and Phil lived in the house that he and Bob built. Although their plan was to only stay on for one or two years, they ended up there much, much longer. The senior Porsilds were fed up with the business when they sold it to Ellen and Phil in May 1965.

"When Phil and I bought the place from my folks, we had two deals, one with my folks that we paid off yearly," Ellen says. "Then we paid off one or two pennies per gallon to White Pass and Yukon Route." They managed to pay off WPYR in eight years.

In the late 1960s, the Davignons paid staff one hundred dollars per month, plus room and board. Most of their staff were high school or college students. They ran the lodge until fall of 1977, when they closed that part of the business down (keeping the rooms for emergency accommodation) and reopened as a bakery and campground. They then paid staff one dollar over minimum wage.

"That bakeshop was such a lucrative business," Ellen says. "We never ran it as a business. The more we sold, the cheaper we sold it for." This point is one Ellen makes often: she didn't run her operations for the purpose of making large profits; she just loved the work. The bakery was so busy that in one summer Ellen used seven tons of flour. The sheer number and variety of baked goods were impressive.

"I'd make twenty-five dozen [three hundred] cinnamon buns a day and a hundred loaves of bread, all the pastries and meat pies," Ellen says. "I first thought I'd bake bread for the store and make cinnamon buns for the people who came looking." Ellen didn't think that after they closed the restaurant people would still come in wanting to order soups and burgers. "I thought cinnamon buns would keep everyone happy, but I wasn't very long in finding that I had to increase my repertoire."

She added meat pies, pizzas, doughnuts, tarts, turnovers and cookies. Because of this increase in baking, she had to start her day at three o'clock in the morning. Mostly, she worked on her own, but sometimes her youngest daughter, Lise, helped.

The few times Ellen took time off from work were for a gallbladder operation and when she gave birth to each of her five children.

In 1992, the Davignons sold Johnson's Crossing to a Fort Nelson construction company, which immediately tripled the campsite prices: fifteen dollars for sites with electricity, ten dollars for sites without.

Johnson's Crossing went through a few more owners and one foreclosure before Sandy and Frank Ruther bought it in January 2014. They re-opened it in June of the same year.

"We're the fifth owners in the life of JC," Sandy says, referring to the lodge by its initialism, as many Yukoners do.

The couple had lived in different places before settling back in the Yukon. They knew about JC from travelling on the highway and living in the community.

"I really don't know what we were thinking when we saw the ad in the realty section," says Frank.

Nowadays Johnson's Crossing is a restaurant and RV park run by Sandy and Frank Ruther. In their pre-JC lives, Sandy ran a "Yukon-famous" burger joint and Frank was a truck driver.

"We're thinking, *Geez, we're kind of bored*," says Sandy.

"We decided to drive down and have a look at it," Frank says. "Then we talked ourselves out of it, then talked ourselves back into it, and here we are."

The Ruthers keep their business open all year round. In the summer, they hire four staff, but in the winter, it's just the two of them.

"The Alaska Highway is pretty quiet in the wintertime," Frank says. "One of us goes to town for groceries, the other one stays."

The Ruthers speak of their business in completely opposite terms from how Ellen Davignon spoke of hers. Sandy worked in the service industry before—she ran Penny's Place, a well-loved burger joint that used to be open in Pelly Crossing, Yukon. Words like "marketing," "planning" and "products" pepper Sandy's sentences.

The couple was initially drawn to the business for the property, but they enjoy the lifestyle: they're busy in the summer but manage at their own pace in the winter.

"In the wintertime, you have a break from the rush of people and it is kind of nice to have time," she says. "And, I get to knit—finish old projects."

Frank and Sandy like the history associated with their property. Frank was a career truck driver and knows the highway well. He has an appreciation for lodges that only those who made their living driving up and down the Alaska Highway can have.

"It's a highway lodge, and they are a dying thing, which is also unique, if you can make a go, even a little bit," Frank says. "It's still a viable service."

Even in their short time running the lodge, they are constantly surprised by the variety in their workdays. "Every day is a new day, and every day is a different day," Frank says.

On one particularly different day, when they first moved into Johnson's Crossing, Frank and Sandy were cleaning up the property and they found a box containing someone's ashes.

"The people who were here before left them [the ashes]," Frank says. "They were supposed to send them back to England. This lady in England was searching for them forever."

The woman's eight-year search ended with Sandy's perseverance to reconnect the urn to a living family member. For clues, she had a number on the box containing the ashes and the name of the crematorium on the bag. "Sandy found the lady in England and they come here last summer," Frank says. "They were so thankful. It was her mother."

Sandy and Frank were also able to give the woman a jewellery box that belonged to the family and had been with the ashes. "The ashes could have been taken out with the trash," Sandy says.

Johnson's Crossing is safe in the hands of Sandy and Frank. They admit living on a remote property is a lifestyle change, but they love running their business together.

"We were just meant to be here," says Sandy. "Despite being a little afraid of doing this, we ended up here."

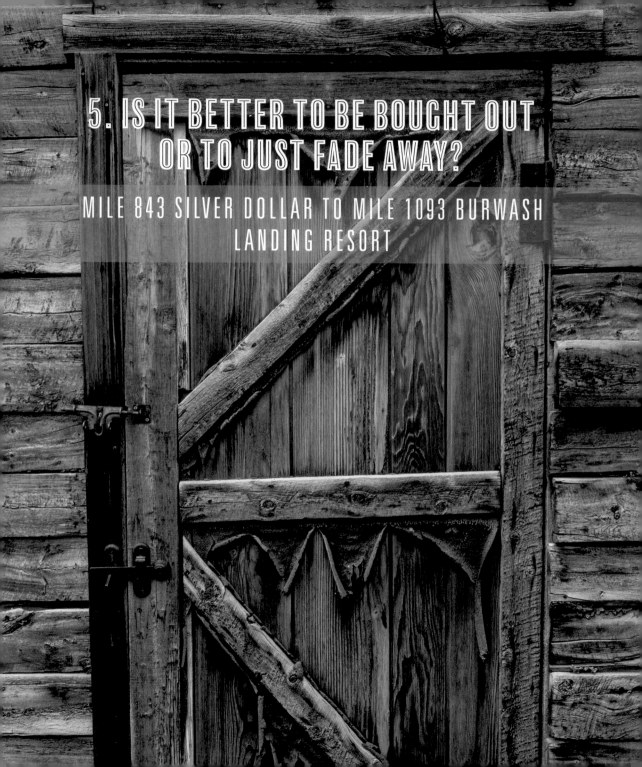

5. IS IT BETTER TO BE BOUGHT OUT OR TO JUST FADE AWAY?

MILE 843 SILVER DOLLAR TO MILE 1093 BURWASH LANDING RESORT

Mile 843 *Silver Dollar*
Mile 866 Jake's Corner
Mile 872 *The Pines / Johnnie's Place*
Mile 883 *Marsh Lake Lodge, aka Mike Nolan's Lodge*
Mile 910 *McCrae Inn*
Mile 918 Whitehorse
Mile 968 *Mendenhall Lodge*
Mile 974 *Harry Chambers's Roadhouse at Champagne*
Mile 988 *Krak-a-Krik or Cracker Creek*
Mile 996 *Canyon Creek*
Mile 1016 Haines Junction Inn / **24**
    Kluane Park Inn
Mile 1022.5 *MacKintosh Trading Post /*
    Bear Creek Lodge
Mile 1054 *Silver Creek Lodge /* **25**
    Kluane Lake Lodge
Mile 1083 Destruction Bay Lodge
Mile 1083 Talbot Arm Motel
Mile 1093 Kluane Lodge/Inn / Burwash **26**
    Landing Resort

Haines Junction is a village that is scattered around the junction where the Alaska Highway makes a sharp right turn and heads northwest toward mainland Alaska. The dead-end Haines Highway, which continues straight ahead going south from that corner, takes the traveller to the coastal village of Haines, Alaska.

Opposite: Silver Creek Lodge was built and run by Johnny Muska, who at one time had a hunting-outfitting business in Burwash Landing.

More than a highway truck stop, Haines Junction has a population of just under six hundred. In the community are housing subdivisions, gas stations, hotels and motels, a grocery store and a liquor store, a school, the über-modern glass-walled Da Kų Cultural Centre and a convention centre, where the annual Kluane Bluegrass Mountain Festival is held each June. This is the start of Kluane country and the traditional territory of Southern Tutchone First Nations. On the west side of the highway is Kluane National Park and Reserve, where you'll find the highest mountains in Canada, which are part of the Saint Elias Mountains. Among these peaks is the tallest mountain in the country: Mount Logan.

The origins of the national park are rooted in controversy. As with the section of the Alaska Highway between Dawson Creek and Fort St. John, long before World War II there was a pre-existing route between Whitehorse and Haines Junction. In 1903, the three-year Kluane gold rush began. Soon, pickaxes, shovels and rocker boxes rattled the Kluane creeks. In response to this new wave of mining, the 134-mile Kluane Wagon Road was built from Whitehorse to Silver City, a now-abandoned trading post north of Haines Junction. The road was completed in 1904, and a trip end to end took travellers a full week.

The construction of the Alaska Highway put hunting pressures on the region and Kluane Game Sanctuary was established in 1943 to protect the wildlife. However, hunting and trapping were banned in the reserve, which meant that First Nations people could not use their traditional territory as they had since time immemorial. This prohibition went on until the ban on hunting and trapping by First Nations people was lifted in 1976, and access was legislated into the land claim agreements of the Kluane First Nation, and the Champagne and Aishihik First Nations, in 2003 and 1993 respectively.

MILE 1016 HAINES JUNCTION INN/ KLUANE PARK INN

THE CONSTRUCTION OF THE Alaska Highway was the historical event that brought the most people into the Kluane area. Haines Junction grew out of the construction and maintenance camps. After the highway opened to the public in 1948, increased population and visitation meant a need for visitor services. Old roadhouses that dated from the early 1900s continued to serve the travellers, and more establishments opened to cater to the newcomers as well.

John and Sally Backe were two people who took advantage of the opportunity brought about by the developing tourism industry. In 1946, they opened a restaurant that they ran out of a wall tent, and

John and Sally Backe opened a restaurant in a wall tent in 1946. This establishment evolved into the Haines Junction Inn which, after a name change in the early 1970s, became the Kluane Park Inn.

The Kluane Park Inn is owned by the Zhu family, who moved from Vancouver in 2012. Ben (pictured) manages the business with his parents. In the tradition of Chinese-Canadian restaurants located in rural Canada, their menu offers a mix of everything from burgers and fries to egg rolls and Szechuan beef.

later they built the Haines Junction Inn. The inn has had a series of different owners, and when in 1974 Neil and Sally Olsen bought it, they renamed it Kluane Park Inn. This name took advantage of the announcement in 1972 of the future establishment of Kluane National Park and the expected rush on tourism.

Sitting near the junction of the Alaska Highway and the Haines Highway, the modern-day Kluane Park Inn, which has a boxy wood-sided first floor exterior and a second floor painted sage green, owes much of its continued operational success to being situated in a community. The owners Jia Sheng "Gary" and Yue Sheng "Sue" Zhu, bought the inn in 2012 and moved from Vancouver to Haines Junction with their eldest son, Ben, to operate the business.

The day's special offers a choice of spaghetti and meat sauce with garlic bread, and the menu includes mainstays of Chinese-Canadian restaurants: burgers, chicken wings, Szechuan beef and egg rolls. Because of the reduction in highway traffic in winter, the restaurant is closed for a couple of months each year. Even the fact of a local community to support the eatery isn't enough in the coldest, darkest parts of winter, though the hotel and bar stay open.

Gary was the first member of the family to travel to the Yukon. He arrived in 2005, to renovate the 202 Motor Inn, which has a bar that is known for having the best dance floor in Whitehorse. The Zhus heard from a friend about the opportunity to buy the inn, and now, here they are: Haines Junction, Yukon. Neither Gary nor Sue is fluent in English, and Ben acts as interpreter and frontline manager.

"I do everything—buy advertising, sign papers," Ben says. "Except the cooking—my dad does the cooking." Ben is a dynamo in his mid-twenties, a born and bred Vancouverite. He is gregarious, talking a mile a minute and exploding with ideas about how he can improve services in his community. He sees a need for a mechanic (with tow truck) to service the highway north of Haines Junction and is trying to convince a friend to move to the Yukon and go into business. Currently, Ben says, there's one mechanic in Haines Junction, who doesn't work weekends; plus, there is only one tow truck, based at Mile 1118, that services the highway between Haines Junction and the US border. As Ben takes payment from a customer for some takeout, he jokes about running for the village council.

In 2016, the Zhus expanded their businesses and bought a local RV park. The family appears to be putting down roots.

"I love it, waking up to the mountains every day," Ben says. "The community is great, people are awesome."

A post of honour: the milepost for the Kluane Park Inn can be found in the bar adjacent to the restaurant.

MILE 1054 SILVER CREEK LODGE/ KLUANE LAKE LODGE

Kluane Experience was a brief-lived business that Michael and Janice Williams opened after the Alaska Highway was rerouted away from their lodge, Kluane Lake Lodge.

AROUND THE TIME CLYDE and Helen Wann were reaching the peak of their highway lodge ownership, another couple was entering highway lodge lore, buying up properties between Haines Junction and Beaver Creek. Conrad and Camilla Bradley were originally from California, and during their time in the Yukon, they owned Mile 1128 Mountain View Lodge, Mile 1167 Rover's Inn and Mile 1169 White River Lodge. Conrad ("Con") and Camilla's then-daughter-in-law, Norma, ran White River Lodge with her husband, Tom, and she convinced her cousin Michael Williams and his wife, Janice, to

move to the Yukon and lease Mile 1128 Mountain View Lodge from Con and Camilla.

"Basically, I was working as a salesman, and I was gone most of the time when the kids were growing up," says Michael. "I decided I didn't want that anymore—I wanted something the whole family could be involved in."

"They [Norma and Tom] said there was money to be made there," adds Janice. "It would be a good living."

The then-twentysomething couple packed up their four kids and belongings in Oregon and headed north, arriving in the Yukon in September 1966. They leased Mountain View Lodge for two years.

"Mountain View was noted for its scenery, supposedly overlooking Mount Logan. That's how they advertised it," Michael says. "But it wasn't Mount Logan you were looking at."

"We had a telescope that looked at the Donjek Range," says Janice. "You put a quarter in and you were able to see the mountains."

Farther north up the highway, at Mile 1118 Mount Kennedy Motel, the then-owner further enhanced the ruse of the view of Mount Logan from the highway, but from his establishment.

"He built up a big, high platform and put a telescope on it and said that you could see the high peaks from his place," says Michael. "He put signs up on the highway advertising that."

The infamous mountain-viewing perch still stands in the parking lot at Mile 1118, but climbing it might be considered a life-endangering act.

The Williamses, who enjoy a wilderness lifestyle, with open spaces, fishing, nature and relative solitude, were very comfortable at Mountain View Lodge. They wanted to buy the property, but they couldn't come to an agreement with Con. They looked at other options.

"We found an abandoned place at Kluane—it was called Silver Creek Lodge at the time," says Michael. "We ended up buying that and re-opened it as Kluane Lake Lodge." That was in 1969.

At the suggestion of a cousin, Michael and Janice Williams moved from Oregon to the Yukon Territory in 1966. They leased Mountain View Lodge for two years before buying Silver Creek Lodge and reopening it as Kluane Lake Lodge in 1969. Currently the lodge is called "Kluane Base Camp" and is owned by Emmanuel and Annie Obeissart.

The previous owner of Silver Creek Lodge had been Johnny Muska, an Albertan who ran an outfitting business in Burwash Landing. He built Silver Creek Lodge in the late 1940s and operated it with his wife. In true country-song fashion, Johnny's wife up and left him, and later in life, he leased out his lodge until he sold it to Michael and Janice Williams.

Expanding on what Johnny offered at Silver Creek, the couple installed a service station and later added a restaurant and rooms.

"It was a Gulf station," says Michael. "We purchased the pumps and paid it off in just over a year. They supplied the pumps and tanks, it was up to us to install them."

"This guy came down from Beaver Creek. He stopped in at White River Lodge for gas, and my Aunt Norma went out to serve him, and he said, 'No woman is going to pump my gas.' So he drove off. My aunt called Pine Valley and said make sure Diane goes out to pump the gas. And the same thing happened there. Then my aunt calls my mom at Mountain View Lodge, and by then he had to get gas."

—Bruce Williams, son of Michael and Janice Williams

The newly named Kluane Lake Lodge was open all year round, but not twenty-four hours a day.

"When someone knocked on the door you answered it," says Janice. "Especially in the winter time, and that did happen now and then, because people would get stranded."

Being a family of six, the Williamses had a built-in workforce to do the chores around the lodge.

"Over the years we did have other people work for us," says Michael. "Mostly for room and board."

"It wasn't like we were looking for people to work for us—it was more like they were looking for a way to stay in the Yukon," says Janice. "They kind of moved in with us."

The Williams children had long commutes to school. When the family lived at Mountain View, Michael and Janice drove the children every weekday thirty-five miles to Burwash Landing, where the kids would take a school bus for another ten miles to the school in Destruction Bay. When the family lived at Kluane Lake Lodge, it was a twenty-nine-mile daily commute to the school in Destruction Bay. In the summer, which was always the busiest season, the children helped out with the lodge.

Other children also lived at the Kluane Lake Lodge in summer. A dark part of recent Canadian history was the government removal of First Nations children from their families. These children were sent to live in other communities, where they'd go to schools and where assimilation into non–First Nation culture and the Christian religion was enforced. In Whitehorse, the capital of the Yukon, the children lived in hostels such as Yukon Hall while they attended day schools. But Yukon Hall closed during the summer, and instead of returning the children to their families, the children went to live with foster families. In the early 1970s, the Williamses were one of those families.

"We started with one, then three, then seven," says Janice. "One year we had twelve, but just in the summertime."

The children came from all over the Yukon: Watson Lake, Carmacks, Pelly Crossing, Whitehorse and even from communities close to the lodge. It's impossible to describe the trauma those children faced in being separated from their families for months or years. Living with the Williams family could in no way replace the children's homes and families, but it offered a respite from the regimented life in the hostel and at the day school.

"We were close to the lake, and across the highway there was a pond where the kids could swim," says Janice. "We had a couple of horses they got to ride. They had our four kids to play with."

Come the start of the school year, the children had to return to Yukon Hall and the drudgery of school.

"When we had to take the kids back, there were a lot of tears," says Janice. "It was hard to take them back, but you were tired by the end of summer. You'd go into that Yukon Hall to visit them, and all the kids would come over, hugging you."

The Williams family operated the lodge until the highway was rerouted away from their business in 1975. A cruel irony was that the construction crew responsible for the realignment of the highway stayed at Micheal and Janice's lodge while they were doing their work. The couple closed Kluane Lake Lodge and moved to Destruction Bay (where they leased the lodge of the same name for one year). They ended up moving back to Kluane Lake to live, but they didn't reopen the lodge.

While the Williams family operated Kluane Lake Lodge, Michael fulfilled his dream of getting a commercial fishing licence, which required that he become a Canadian citizen. Michael operated a commercial fishing business, netting whitefish and lake trout from Kluane Lake and selling his catch along the highway from Haines Junction to Beaver Creek. He continued doing this after the couple left the lodge business.

"We started a whitefish market," Janice says. "The natives were eating it, but no one else."

Michael's business partner was Richard Mazur (who ran Kluane Park Inn in Haines Junction at the time), and they divided the work between them. Richard had contacts in the businesses along the highway and he'd take the orders. Michael caught and prepared the fish into steaks or filets, ready to be smoked or cooked, then delivered it to the customer.

"From Kluane Lake Lodge, I always did it in the wintertime when things were slow," Michael says. "I'd fish through the ice, and when we didn't have the lodge, I did it full time."

Their fish travelled as far as to customers in Vancouver.

"We had a bus driver from Vancouver, and he would take our whitefish frozen to Vancouver," says Janice, "and he had a guy who'd sell it down there."

In 1996, Michael and Janice sold the property, then they moved to Oregon, but their years in the Yukon are never far from their thoughts.

"It was an experience," says Michael. "It was a lot of work without a lot of return sometimes. What you made in the summer got you through the winter, sometimes, if you were lucky. It was a good life."

MILE 1093 KLUANE INN/LODGE / BURWASH LANDING RESORT

LURED BY THE RICH PROMISES of the Klondike gold rush, in 1898 brothers Eugene ("Gene") and Louis Jacquot left the vineyard-filled valleys of the Lorraine region in northeast France for the Yukon Territory. From the Klondike, the brothers pursued the Kluane gold rush and settled on the shore of Kluane Lake, where they established a trading post in an area that was a traditional First Nations seasonal fishing camp. At that time, to access the Jacquot brothers' post from Whitehorse, travellers needed to take the wagon road to Silver City, and then go by boat across Kluane Lake to reach Burwash Landing. (The landing was named after Lachlan Burwash, who was the mining recorder at Silver City.)

When Gertrude Baskine, the intrepid "hitchhiker," arrived in Burwash Landing in 1943, she wrote, "At the very first view, I lost my heart to the place." Much to Gertrude's disappointment, the White River had washed out the Alaska Highway and her trip was delayed. She spent weeks as a guest of the Jacquots as she waited to traverse

This photo of the newly built Kluane Inn was taken by Bob Porsild, who was hired by the Jacquots to build the inn over the winter of 1946/47.
Photo by Bob Porsild, courtesy of Ellen Davignon.

Opposite: The now-closed Burwash Landing Resort commands a stunning view of Kluane Lake.

the river. Besides operating the trading post, the brothers also guided and mined in the area.

Three years after Gertrude's visit, the Jacquot brothers hired a man to build the Kluane Inn, which was referred to as either an "inn" or a "lodge" in different publications. The person they found was Robert ("Bob") Porsild, who later built and operated Mile 836.5 Johnson's Crossing Lodge, which explains the similarity in appearance of the two lodges (though the original lodge at Johnson's Crossing has since been dismantled). Within a year, Gene and his wife, Ruth (née Dickson), were running their new business. The Alaska Highway AAA spring 1950 guide described the Kluane Inn as having nineteen rooms and four showers. A single would set a guest back $2.50, and a double was $2 more. The establishment was described as "very comfortable."

The Jacquots ran the lodge until Gene's death in 1950, and then Ruth sold it to Leland Allinger and Darrell Duensing, who changed the name to Burwash Landing Resort in the 1960s. The business partners added to the lodge, renovating it and building it up until 1982, when

they sold it to Ollie Wirth and his business partner, Chris Modersohn; the latter left the partnership and was replaced by Roy Oliver one year later.

The lodge remained open and was operated by Ollie and his wife, Helen, until 2013, when they sold it to the Kluane Community Development Corporation (KCDC). Since then, the business has been closed, and it remains to be seen what will happen to the property, which has a breathtaking view of Kluane Lake.

"Historic Building May Fall to 'Dozer's Blade" was the title of the article by Christopher Reynolds in the January 6, 2015, edition of the *Whitehorse Star*, the only daily newspaper in the Yukon. The building under threat was the Burwash Landing Resort. According to the

Ollie and Helen Wirth ran Burwash Landing Resort for thirty-one years. They miss the heyday of lodge ownership and mourn the closure of the lodge in 2013.

article, Kluane First Nation held community meetings to discuss the future of the resort. Then-chief Mathieya Alatini was quoted as saying, "the decision to bulldoze the building was 'unanimous' among the shareholders Kluane citizens."

After Ollie and Helen sold the resort and the accompanying 57-hectare (140-acre) property, they moved to Haines Junction, seventy-two miles southeast of Burwash Landing. In August of 2015, in the bar of the Kluane Park Inn in Haines Junction, seventy-four-year-old Ollie sat on a barstool, adamant that the KCDC promised to keep the resort open.

With Ollie's remarkably white chin-curtain beard, at the turn of another century, he could be mistaken for a Mennonite--if it weren't for his gold nugget ring and watch strap, and brilliant white ballcap. The gleaming black bartop reflected the paper currency of various denominations from different countries taped to the wall. The question lingered in the air: Who could fault the KCDC for wanting to own a sizeable piece of prime realty within its traditional territory and doing with it as they saw fit? And weren't Ollie and Helen fortunate to find a buyer for their thirty-one-year investment when lodges in various states of disrepair were for sale or abandoned all along the highway?

One of the oldest lodges along the Alaska Highway, the now-closed Burwash Landing Resort was opened by the Jacquot family in 1947.
Yukon Archives, Elmer Harp Jr. fonds, 2006/2, #366.

"I'm really sorry that I sold the place," Ollie said. Seated beside him was Helen, a youthful-looking woman with a sparkle in her eyes that rivalled the twinkle of the metallic flecks in the bartop.

"We left everything behind," she said. "All they had to do was turn the key."

Lodge owners such as Ollie and Helen often talk about the good old days, when business was hopping and tour bus passengers filled dining halls and rooms. When asked what he thought had changed over the years, Ollie's answer reflected the sad conundrum that many small towns and remote communities across Canada and the United States face.

"There are no more bonspiels, no more things for the community happen," Ollie said. "We used to have the outfitters' ball, now it's gone to Whitehorse. The local people here die off and the old traditions die. The new generation just don't keep up with the old traditions."

The heyday of the Alaska Highway lodges was an era of unpaved roads, gas-guzzling vehicles, tour bus traffic and costly airfare. The twenty-first century is a striking contrast, with a paved and chip-sealed highway, fuel-efficient vehicles, fewer tour buses and airlines offering more affordable flights.

In the 1980s, Helen baked forty pies daily. "We'd have seventeen buses per day for lunch at the Your Place café," Helen said. The couple also had a gas station, restaurant and hotel on their property. "We had twenty-two staff at one point."

The Wirths adapted their lodge to changes in highway traffic. They built an RV park and arranged fishing trips and flight tours over the glaciers in Kluane National Park and Reserve. Then the 1980 recession hit. "Tourism is dead," Ollie is quoted as saying in a research paper that explores the evolution of the tourism and accommodation trade and its connection to the development of Kluane National Park and Reserve, as well as the influence that park regulations had on the businesses. Rebecca Burton, the author of the paper, interviewed Ollie in December 1996, and at that time his business had been closed for the third winter in a row.

Sometimes the picture in the rearview mirror is rose tinted. As of the end of August 2016, Burwash Landing Resort was still standing on the shore of Kluane Lake, empty and a bit more weatherworn than when the Wirths ran it.

6. TOWARD THE BORDER

MILE 1095 JOE'S AIRPORT TO MILE 1220 PIONEER INN

Mile 1095 Joe's Airport
Mile 1118 Kluane Wilderness Village and 27
Mile 1118 Café and Scully's Saloon
Mile 1128 Mountain View Lodge 28
Mile 1147 Pine Valley Lodge / 29
Pine Valley Bakery and Lodge
Mile 1156 Northland
Mile 1164 Cook's Koidern River Lodge 30
Mile 1167 (west side) Bear Flats Lodge 31
Mile 1167 (east side) Rover's Inn
Mile 1169 White River Lodge / 32
Discovery Yukon Lodgings
Mile 1184 Dry Creek
Mile 1188 Ingel or Engel Lake Lodge
Mile 1202 Beaver Creek Lodge / Alas/Con 33
Border Lodge / Westmark Beaver Creek /
Beaver Creek RV Park and Motel
Mile 1219 Sourdough Roadhouse
Mile 1220 Pioneer Inn

Previous page: Little remains of Mountain View Lodge at Mile 1128.

Legend has it that, until the 2000s, between Mile 1059 and the Yukon–Alaska border, highway lodge owners made their own rules and didn't care what anyone thought of it. It was the Mildly Wild West. One lodge owner pelted rocks at the vehicles of tourists he didn't like. More than twenty years after the sale of one lodge, the current owner still owes $2,000 to the previous owner. Two lodge owners shot at each other, sabotaged each other's businesses and went to court over a variety of contentious issues. Suspicious fires were lit, perhaps connected to the two rival lodge owners. Lodges burned down. One lodge operated as a brothel. Another rumour implies collusion and collaboration: two lodge owners a mere twenty-five miles apart would put up *Road Washed Out* signs on the highway to keep people staying at their lodges one or two days more. Truth or rumour, a certain lawless mischief infused that section of the highway.

> "[At Mile 1118,] one of the guys from the service station came running over in the middle of the night and said, 'They're killing the bartender.' It was just a party that went a little awry. Dad took his shotgun, and he did let off a shot and cleared the bar. He did get a severe warning from the RCMP, that that was an unacceptable way to convey a message."
> —Terri Trout, daughter of John Trout, owner (with his wife, Liz) of the Kluane Wilderness Village and Mile 1118 Café and Scully's Saloon from 1972 to 2004

There are no communities, and only one lodge and some private and Yukon government campgrounds, operating on the 109-mile section of road between Burwash Landing and the community of Beaver Creek (Mile 1202) near the Yukon–Alaska border. As mentioned earlier, the only tow truck between the two villages is located at Mile 1118, the now-closed Kluane Wilderness Village. As you drive this section of road, it feels somewhat post-apocalyptic. Not that the landscape is scarred by fire or destroyed by bombs, but you'll pass few vehicles in either direction, and most of the buildings you drive by are abandoned lodges. It's a stark contrast to the 1970s and 1980s, when, it's said, a cook served fifty gallons of soup to twenty tour buses for lunch. One lodge rented out cabins for eight-hour shifts. Another lodge was so busy that a person could literally walk from RV roof to RV roof in the campground.

MILE 1118 KLUANE WILDERNESS VILLAGE AND SCULLY'S SALOON AND CAFÉ

IN 1972, JOHN TROUT MOVED from Alberta to the Yukon to buy Mile 1118, the site of the former Mount Kennedy Motel, which had previously burned down. A perfectly situated lodge, Kluane Wilderness Village (KWV) was roughly two hundred miles east from Tok, Alaska, and two hundred miles west from Whitehorse, Yukon. It was the ideal place for tour buses to stop for lunch. John ran the lodge with his wife, Liz Trout (previously Waine), and had a business partner, Joseph Frigon, who lived in Edmonton.

The five Trout-Waine children spent their first summer together at KWV in 1975: Terri, Don and Jay Trout flew from Edmonton, and the Waine children, Brendan and Andrea, flew from Vancouver. Terri was ten years old at the time and has vivid memories of the shocking difference between home in Edmonton and her new summer home in the Yukon, where there was no running water and very few people.

"It was scary," Terri says. "It was a really different living circumstance coming from Edmonton. The highway was a lot different then—it was in horrible shape, really bad potholes and tons of construction."

As they drove from Whitehorse, they passed through Haines Junction at two o'clock in the morning and arrived at the lodge in the early hours. "It seemed like it was so far away," Terri says. "That ended up becoming our grocery run later on when we were adults."

Both John and Liz worked full time to keep the lodge running, and the five children kept themselves entertained. "We found a place to fish and we saw gophers," Terri says. "When we were kids, we were fearless." The children would often overnight in the woods and spend their days at a swimming hole half a mile down the road. "Just playing away. My dad always said that we made too much noise, and the bears would never have anything to do with us."

All the Trout-Waine children worked at the lodge, usually starting with dishwashing. Terri's first full-time shift was when she was about thirteen. She ended up working mostly in the restaurant, though she cleaned rooms as well. Terri last worked at the lodge in 2002.

Terri describes her father as driven and energetic. "He was funny and was either yelling or dancing, singing, telling jokes. He really was a salesman at heart, and he looked at Kluane Wilderness Village

Ron Edinger was a long-time employee of John and Liz Trout. He is now part-owner of their property and runs a tow-truck and mechanic service from Mile 1118.

Scully's Saloon's namesake George Scullen moved with his wife, Helen, to Mile 1118 in the early 1980s. A talented woodworker, George a.k.a. "Scully" made the burl bar that was the centrepiece of Scully's Saloon. "Scully was quite a drawing card for people to come to the lodge," says Terri Trout, daughter of John Trout. "He used to make bowls and clocks out of burls, and then later on he would just sell the burls."

as such a huge challenge and adventure and just fell in love with all the people up there."

John was drawn to gold mining, and in the last decade of his life, he pursued his mining interests in the Fortymile area and turned over the management of the lodge to his son Don. Following John's death in 2004, Don continued to operate the lodge, but he ran into a problem that has plagued numerous lodges along the highway: sanitation. The course of the river had changed over the years and was too close to the septic field. The government required a new one to be built, but the cost was prohibitive.

When Terri's father and stepmother ran the lodge, the sense of community was strong along the highway. Each lodge or community in the area would host a special event: a fishing derby and dance in Destruction Bay in July, a solstice party in Burwash Landing, the Miners' Ball at Kluane Wilderness Village, a motorcycle rally at Pine Valley Lodge. It is that sense of friendship and support, as well as the great outdoors, that made a lasting impression on Terri.

"It was such a fabulous place to spend the summers. You'd wake up in the mornings with the mountains out the front door, the river out the back door, the creek and the lake just down the road for walking," she says. "As a city girl, I was always in awe."

The lodge has been closed since 2005. Former employee and now co-owner Ron Edinger lives with his two dogs on the property (Liz Trout and Ellie Frigon are the other co-owners). He provides automotive and tow truck services along the highway between Haines Junction and the Canada–US border. The twisted and bent remains of numerous vehicles in front of the garage and lodge attest to the need for Ron's services.

Ron was working in the logging industry when he heard that John Trout was looking to hire a mechanic. He applied and got the job,

Mile 1118 Café and Scully's Saloon was torn down in 2016. A bulldozer removed the lumber and the memorabilia, like this Polaroid, that used to decorate the legendary watering hole.

and has been at KWV ever since. "I left for one year in the eighties," he says. Since Scully's Saloon at Mile 1118 was torn down in the summer of 2016, and Kluane Wilderness Village closed, Ron has only one plan for the future. "Going to be here till the end." Whenever or whatever that may mean.

A tow truck mirror reflects the scenery near Kluane Wilderness Village.

MILE 1128 MOUNTAIN VIEW LODGE

BY NOW YOU'LL BE FAMILIAR with the surnames Wann, Bradley and Steele—people who were truly invested in the economy of the Alaska Highway lodges. As we approach the Yukon–Alaska Border, Wann and Bradley show up again. The various places people moved from to operate lodges might have your head spinning. Hang on, 'cause here we go.

In 1961, Sid van der Meer was twenty-four years old when he travelled from Alberta to the Yukon with a friend to "come have a look." Fifty-six years later, after working in a number of lodges and a brief stint living "outside" the territory, he makes his home in Beaver Creek, Yukon. Here he's a mere thirty-five miles north of the first lodge he worked at that summer of 1961: Mile 1167 Rover's Inn. "I

Sid van der Meer worked at Mountain View Lodge for many years before he bought the lodge from his employer Conrad Bradley. The two men confirmed the sale with a handshake.

was working in construction in Edmonton, and this guy had a lodge on the Alaska Highway and needed someone to run it," Sid says. The story continues that the guy gave Sid a letter to take to the Bank of Montreal in Whitehorse to get money for the renovations of the lodge. When Sid arrived at the bank, it turned out that that guy owed money to the bank, but Sid ended up working at the lodge just the same. Sid and his friend were supposed to manage the Rover's Inn together, but when his friend's wife arrived two weeks later, she was not impressed, and the couple decamped immediately back to Vancouver. The inn was a mess.

"We couldn't even run the pumps," Sid says. "We got a fill-up of fuel from White Pass, but it was spilling everywhere."

Sid gave up on the inn and went to work as a handyman for Con and Camilla Bradley, who had built Mile 1128 Mountain View Lodge, which consisted of three cabins, a service station, a grocery store and small living quarters.

"I did whatever—pumped gas, fixed tires, fixed cars. We had a tow truck and we picked wrecks off the road. I did everything."

Con and Camilla increased their business holdings in 1962, when they bought Mile 1169 White River Lodge from Danny Nowlan, but they still owned Mountain View Lodge and needed someone to run it. Off the Bradleys drove back to California to see if they could wrangle some relatives into the gig. That is how their son Tom, his then-wife, Norma, and their three children moved to the Yukon in 1962.

"It was an eye-opener," says Norma White on the phone from her present home in Idaho. "We had zero experience in operating a business of any kind." Norma and Tom ended up running White River Lodge just the same.

This is where the chart would come in handy. If you recall, Tom and Norma convinced her cousin Michael Williams and his wife, Janice, to move to the Yukon to run Mountain View Lodge in 1966. By the end of the 1960s, the senior Bradleys and their extended family had a quiet monopoly over lodges from Haines Junction to Beaver Creek.

Much like the community between Haines Junction and Mile 1118, the people of the close-knit lodge community between Mile 1118 and the border spent a lot of time travelling between lodges and visiting with one another. There were dances, bonspiels, parties. One ill-fated night in 1963, Sid was visiting friends at the Rover's Inn when it met a fiery end and burned to the ground.

"I was there in front of the building, throwing everything out the window, 'til someone yelled, 'Get out!'"

In the late 1960s, Con and Camilla were getting ready to retire, and one day, Con told Sid that he was going to sell the Mile 1128 Mountain View Lodge to Sid and his then-wife, Marilyn.

"I starts laughing and I says, 'Con, I've been working for you for all these years, you know how much you've been paying me. You know I don't have any goddamn money,'" Sid says.

The two men settled the deal with a handshake in 1968: $10,000 paid off in yearly $1,000 installments. Con and Camilla moved back to California, where he died of cancer seven years later. The van der Meers ran the lodge for nine years before deciding to sell because their children were attending school in Destruction Bay, forty-five miles south, and the drive was too difficult.

"We sold it all and went to Alberta for a few years," says Sid. "I bought a pool hall, grocery store, restaurant, and run that for a few years and moved back up here again."

Back at Mile 1128, there is very little left of the lodge. The man who bought it from the van der Meers bulldozed the buildings to make way for a new construction that was never built. "There's one cabin left and half a cabin back in the bush," Sid says. He keeps the original milepost for Mile 1128 on the front deck of his home in Beaver Creek.

Sid moved back to Beaver Creek in 1996 and eventually took up the job of supervisor at the Yukon Visitor Information Centre, where he's worked for sixteen years. This was another happenstance employment opportunity.

"One of the girls quit or something halfway through the season, and I was hanging around there a lot anyway, and they asked me if I wanted to work there, and I said yes."

Sid says he's been approached to buy back Mile 1128, but it wouldn't be to operate a lodge.

"You couldn't do it anymore with all the rules, codes, septic. It'd cost a million dollars to open up."

Mountain View Lodge was demolished decades ago, and only a couple of cabins from the lodge remain at Mile 1128.

MILE 1147 PINE VALLEY BAKERY AND LODGE/ PINE VALLEY LODGE

MILE 1147 PINE VALLEY BAKERY and Lodge sits on the east side of a short straight stretch of highway. Spruce trees border the parking lot and the back side of the property. The tidy log buildings are painted the colour of dark chocolate. The owners, Olivier and Mylène Le Diuzet, immigrated from France in the early 2000s, and in 2009 bought the business, changing the name slightly to reflect Olivier's previous career as a baker. The couple had a lot of work ahead of them when they took over the lodge.

Opposite: An old cabin hides among the spruce trees and fireweed at Pine Valley Bakery.

Below: The tidy log structures of Pine Valley Bakery and Lodge reflect the hard work of new owners.

"It looked like Koidern, inside and out," Olivier says, referring to the dilapidated Mile 1164 Cook's Koidern Lodge (CKL), which was built in 1969 and had been operated by Jim and Dorothy Cook, more sporadically in recent years, until Jim's death over the winter of 2014–15. The CKL yard is littered with vehicles in various states of rust and disrepair, the burgundy paint on the building has faded and the gas pumps register prices from a previous decade, even though the lodge officially closed in 2015. There is a *For Sale* sign posted on the gas station.

"We had to make over a hundred trips to the dump," says Olivier of their first few months as owners of the Pine Valley Bakery and Lodge.

A broken-down car, a dilapidated cabin and old signs combine to create a time capsule of another era at Pine Valley Bakery and Lodge.

The local Yukon newspapers report the lengthy struggle the Le Diuzets have had regarding sanitation with territorial government departments, which forced them to keep their lodge closed for a few years. Finally, their troubles are resolved, and the Pine Valley Bakery and Lodge is open for business. In the summer, visitors to the bright dining room can enjoy unusual highway fare: homemade quiche, crepes, bread and fruit tarts. In the off-season, the couple close shop to make the most of the natural setting of their isolated woodland paradise.

Pine Valley Motel was built during the 1960s tourism operation boom by Jerry and Diane Mogensen, who stuck it out through the 1980s. Finally, in 1989, Jerry sold the business to Carmen Hinson.

Carmen Hinson gained notoriety after the song "Buckshot Betty" was penned in her honour by Yukon singer-songwriter Barbara Chamberlin.

According to Carmen, Jerry basically just decided that she would buy the lodge from him, as he was ready to retire.

By that time, Carmen had a seventeen-year connection with highway lodge culture. Her family had moved to the Yukon when she was a child, and her father was a truck driver who worked with highway maintenance. It is his fault that, at the impressionable age of twelve, she caught the highway lodge bug at Mile 710 Rancheria Lodge.

Pine Valley Bakery and Lodge retains its old-time highway lodge charm with typical decor: antlers above the door.

"My dad dropped me off and said, 'Go work.'" Her employers were Doris and Bud Simpson. "It was kind of cool—there was a bar right next to where my room was. There, they'd leave the back door open, and the truckers would come in and cook their [own] dinner, and leave money in a tin."

Later, Carmen worked at Kluane Wilderness Village and was leasing the café at Pine Valley Lodge in the early 1980s when Jerry decided he wanted to sell the lodge to her.

"I was left with a broken screwdriver and a wrench, that was about it," Carmen says. "He had a couple of old generators there. It was one of those Whitey's 7kW that you got to crank it, and an old Cat motor generator—you gotta start that one first and get the other one going."

The electrical wiring at the lodge was so creative that if the coffee pot was plugged in, nothing else could be.

When Carmen bought the lodge, she wasn't a carpenter, but she learned how to be one—and an electrician and a welder. She then trained to be a welder, and after she closed the lodge for the summer in September, she worked in the oil patch during the winter. She developed a reputation for toughness and wherewithal, which is immortalized in Yukon singer-songwriter Barb Chamberlin's song "The Ballad of Buckshot Betty."

"It's about me, and it's all true," says Carmen.

The rocking blues song tells the tale of Buckshot Betty, a five-foot-two frontier heroine who bakes with butter, hunts for her supper, dances on the table, makes home brew and has an encounter with a grizzly bear that ends with the bear hightailing it back to the woods.

Carmen's spring opener motorcycle rally also became infamous for its size and wildness. The Tundra Tramps motorcycle club would ride from Whitehorse, and the Pan Handlers, a club from Juneau, would arrive via ferry at Haines, Alaska, and whoever else had a motorcycle would meet at Pine Valley Lodge. Entertainment included mud wrestling and performances by "Tagish" Elvis A. Presley—the self-proclaimed real King of Rock 'n' Roll. The CIA, the FBI and aliens have something to do with his claim. He dresses like the King, and on a dark, foggy night looks passably like him. To judge for yourself, you can watch his appearance on *Dragons' Den* in episode 11, season 8, during which Tagish was seeking an investor to partner on his modest merchandise and personal appearance "empire." Carmen says: "Tagish, he'd show up in his pink Cadillac, I'd have the drums going. Everybody loved it." Carmen threw her annual fiesta for three or four years.

After selling Pine Valley Lodge, Carmen moved farther northwest to Beaver Creek and opened Buckshot Betty's, but this business is now for sale. After decades of working in lodges, she's not sure what she'll do if the property sells.

"I like Vegas," she says mischievously, implying she might be leaving the work behind, but she's not about to abandon the fun.

LITRES

$160
PER LTR

$ PRICE INCLUDING TAXES

Unoccupied lodges such as Cook's Koidern River Lodge (above) and Bear Flats Lodge (right) are often a mix of disused fuel pumps and tanks, rusted and broken-down vehicles, old tires and buildings inhabited by mice and squirrels.

MILE 1169 DISCOVERY YUKON LODGINGS/ WHITE RIVER LODGE

When Amanda Harris became the owner of White River Lodge, she renamed it Discovery Yukon Lodgings, but kept up the eclectic taxidermy and knick-knack collection.

AFTER CROSSING THE BRIDGE over the wide and braided, silty White River, the Alaska Highway continues to swoop in a gentle bend to the left. At Mile 1169, on the west side of the highway, lies an expanse of well-manicured lawn. It holds an appropriate number of evergreens standing tall, pleasing to the eye; a few strategically placed US Army vehicles of 1940s vintage; and a single-level bungalow-style

building—the main office. On the western side of the property is an airstrip that could easily pass for a golf driving range, and past the RV sites sit small log cabins and a cluster of white wall tents. The site is without gas pumps and a garage, but there is the hum of a generator. This distinct vacation oasis, a notch above the average Yukon gravel-pad RV and camping sites, is Discovery Yukon Lodgings (DYL). When nature's greenery is at its late-August peak, the whole scene sparkles like an emerald in the midmorning sun.

Amanda Harris, a landed immigrant who made her way to Canada from England via Ireland, has been operating DYL since 2008. It is her old-world country-garden aesthetic that makes DYL a visual

The history of the Alaska Highway is honoured at Discovery Yukon Lodgings with an informal outdoor museum that includes vintage US Army trucks and a vast collection of old-school chainsaws.

standout in the territory. Before it was DYL, it was White River Lodge, and before that it was the basecamp of Utah Construction, one of the companies contracted by the US Army to build the highway.

According to Rebecca Burton's research paper on tourism north of Haines Junction, Mr. and Mrs. Gloslee opened Mile 1169 White River Lodge in the mid-1950s. The couple inherited the Quonset huts that had been used to house US Army engineer troops and then Utah Construction crews. The main building had six officers' rooms.

One of the subsequent owners, Danny Nowlan, ran the tire shop and gas station, and his wife, Erica, ran the restaurant and lodge. Danny and Erica hosted many different people at their lodge— including RCMP officers who often travelled the route.

"There was a former RCMP member who came by who had been based in Haines Junction, and he said they didn't get any per diem at the time," Amanda says. The RCMP had to patrol the highway from Haines Junction to the border and back again. "He'd slept on the couch here many a night." The man couldn't remember the name of the owner at the time, but he said the owner had the same hairstyle as Elvis. When Amanda showed him a picture of Danny, the man said, "That was him."

Danny sold the lodge to Con and Camilla Bradley, and then he moved to Whitehorse and opened the Yukon Game Farm, which evolved into the Yukon Wildlife Preserve. When the senior Bradleys purchased White River Lodge, some of the lodgings were a little primitive.

"The rooms in the lodge were where the horses were kept during the building of the highway," says Norma White, who ran the lodge from 1962 to 1986 with her former husband, Tom Bradley, son of Con and Camilla. "Needless to say, there was much renovation done over the years."

When Norma White and her then-husband Tom Bradley owned the lodge, they had six children who attended school in Beaver

A two-room outhouse offers a gentle warning to users.

Creek, a daily one-way, thirty-mile commute to the north during the school year.

"Truly it was a wonderful place to raise children," she says. "But long, hard hours—fourteen to sixteen hours per day, seven days per week—was the bad part."

Norma says running the lodges was unlike anything else she'd experienced.

"I had to learn how to cook," says Norma. "It was pretty much sink or swim, so we learned how to swim well."

Norma and Tom operated the lodge jointly until they divorced in 1986, after which Norma remained at the lodge for a time but then leased the management to others until she sold the property in 1990.

Although the Bradleys moved away from White River Lodge more than twenty-five years ago, their legacy lives on with the cabins they built in the 1960s and the impressive taxidermy and antique knick-knack collection in the DYL reception building.

"It was kept up by the Beatties and is still owned by them," Amanda says. The military vehicles belong to her, though. "I thought I'd have to keep it [the Alaska Highway military theme] up."

Robert and Caulene Beatty ran the lodge twenty-four hours a day, year round, and had a staff of fifteen people at their busiest times. Things changed when they bought a business in British Columbia, and after that they ran White River Lodge only in the summer.

Amanda and her former husband were on an extended vacation when they found White River Lodge in the summer of 2006.

"We came here on holiday with an RV, and the place was for sale," Amanda says. "We were looking at a place in Peru, and a place on the Alaska side of the border in the same mountain range, then came down here, and here I am."

Amanda and her husband separated, and he remains in Ireland. She moved to Beaver Creek in January of 2008, and it took her awhile to adjust to the cold. When she took over the lodge, she realized she had a lot of work ahead of her. The first task was renovating the kitchen, which had been condemned.

Mileposts are rare souvenirs from pre-metric conversion days, and Discovery Yukon Lodgings' owner Amanda Harris has hung on to the original Mile 1169 White River Lodge milepost.

"You'd lift the floorboards, and it wasn't just those that were rotten, it was the joists as well," she says. "You think it's just a little job... Everything took so much longer than I thought it would take."

Over the years, Mile 1169 has hosted various highway maintenance and mining exploration crews. It was a man from one of these crews who saved DYL from what could have been disaster. In June 2016, Amanda was woken up at two o'clock in the morning by a knocking at her door. She thought someone must've seen a bear, but it turned out that her generator was on fire.

By a stroke of strange luck, Amanda kept a drum of fuel in the generator shed. "The lid blew on it, and it blew the roof out and the heat got out of the building," Amanda says. "The heat was so intense and we couldn't get close to it."

A call to the fire department in Beaver Creek went unanswered.

Amanda and her staff used the garden hoses to try to douse the flames, and then one of them remembered that the man running the water truck on the highway crew was staying in one of the cabins. He got his water truck and poured all the water around the base of the fire.

"The place was full of RVs—we had to wake them up and get them to move, just in case," Amanda says. "We were so lucky. Nobody was hurt and we didn't lose the fuel tank."

What she did lose was her main and backup generators, a ride-on lawnmower and landscaping equipment. The loss of a generator at an off-grid lodge is enormous: the generator is what keeps everything running, including fridges, stoves, lighting and campsite power. "People don't understand about generators," she says. "Someone

White River Lodge began as a camp for Utah Construction during the construction phase of the Alaska Highway. Pictured is an original company truck.

asked one of the staff the other day if that motor [the generator] is to scare the bears away."

DYL was without electricity for a few days, which had an effect on business. "We lost a lot of reservations, but some people were happy with it—we gave a discount."

Amanda adds this hard-learned lesson to a long and growing list of learning experiences: "You don't put your main and backup genera-tor in the same building."

She operates her business from May to the end of September; then she heads to the Sunshine Coast to be closer to where her son is attending university. She hates to leave, but it's also hard for her to be far from her son. Amanda explains that running the lodge has challenged her in ways she hadn't expected.

"I thought I knew what I was made of when I came here, but I find out more," she says. "I thought I'd seen it all, then there was the fire—I had no experience of fire."

MILE 1202 BEAVER CREEK LODGE / ALAS/CON BORDER / WESTMARK BEAVER CREEK LODGE / BEAVER CREEK RV PARK AND MOTEL

Opposite: Beat and Jyl Ledergerber reopened Beaver Creek RV Park and Motel in 2014. The couple has seen a steady increase in business since then.

BORDER TOWNS ARE OFTEN DESCRIBED as raucous, noto-rious, nefarious. Beaver Creek, Yukon, population 103, is none of these things. You won't miss it if you blink, but if you yawn, you just might. Located at Mile 1202 on the Alaska Highway, the village of Beaver Creek is in the territory of the White River First Nation, tra-ditional speakers of the Athapaskan languages Northern Tutchone, a language that spreads to the south, and Upper Tanana, which crosses over the Canada–US border into Alaska. The village itself grew out

of the necessity the highway brought with its completion in 1942: the customs office, an inn, a store, a lodge, a school and so on.

It's almost impossible to talk about lodges along the Alaska Highway without repeatedly mentioning Clyde Wann—a businessman and entrepreneur who has appeared in this book several times already. As described, he was an American prospector from the

Beaver Creek Lodge was built by Clyde and Helen Wann. According to Gordon Steele, whose father, Frank, was Clyde's business partner for a time, this lodge was Helen's "baby."

lower forty-eight who travelled north to Alaska, then east to Yukon. He became known as the "father of Yukon aviation" when he and two business partners started Yukon Airways and Exploration, the first commercial airline in the territory.

But Clyde's entrepreneurship didn't end with aviation. The completion of the Alaska Highway and the opening of it to the public in 1948 was no doubt part of his inspiration to broaden his business interests to include Alaska Highway lodges. He built Mile 733.4 Swift River Lodge, Mile 777.7 Morley River Lodge, Mile 1083 Destruction Bay Lodge and Mile 1202 Beaver Creek Lodge.

Of his four lodges, only one is in operation today. The original Mile 1083 Destruction Bay Lodge was destroyed by fire, as was the original Mile 777.7 Morley River in 1952, which was then rebuilt but is now closed. Mile 733.4 Swift River has been shuttered for a few years. Mile 1202 Beaver Creek Lodge, which was built in 1954, was closed briefly in 2013 but is experiencing a revival since Beat and Jyl Ledergerber bought it in 2014.

"Clyde was a good old soul—a hard-working man," says Ellen Davignon, who ran Mile 836.5 Johnson's Crossing Lodge. "He'd have circles under his eyes down to his belly button, he'd be so tired."

Ellen's father, Bob, who built and ran Johnson's Crossing Lodge before her, bought fuel from Clyde until the two had a disagreement. "Clyde and Dad couldn't keep their accounting straight," she says. "They came to verbal blows, and then Dad made a deal with White Pass and Yukon Route."

By all accounts, Clyde was a driven and resourceful man, but losing business to his rival, WPYR—which he competed against in aviation (for a short time), accommodation and fuel—must've smarted.

Although Beaver Creek Lodge was the last lodge that Clyde built, its reputation as a fine establishment was mostly because of his wife Helen's efforts.

"Helen ran Beaver Creek, that was her lodge," says Gordon Steele, whose father, Frank, was Clyde's business partner for many years. Gordon's parents were lifelong friends of the Wanns. "She [Helen] really didn't like Clyde there [at Beaver Creek Lodge]. He'd always end up firing the cooks, then he'd take over and he couldn't cook worth a damn."

An article by Stanton H. Patty in the July 16, 1956, edition of the *Seattle Times* described the lodge as having wall panelling made of mahogany from the Philippines and noted that a "cheery fire burns in the stone fireplace of the lobby." At the time of Stanton's visit, the lodge was open all year and was more isolated than it is now. The Wanns' closest neighbours were twenty-five miles away, and once a week a truck coming from White-horse delivered "canned goods, potatoes and other provisions."

In 1966, just a year before Clyde died, the Wanns sold the lodge to Westours Bus Company, and the name was changed to Alas/Con Lodge. The tour bus company was absorbed into Holland America and, as the West-

When Beaver Creek Lodge was first opened, it was known for its mahogany panelling and stone fireplace in the lobby.

mark Beaver Creek, the lodge provided accommodation for the tour buses for decades. From the early 1990s onwards, the lodge was known within the bus tour itinerary for a gold rush–themed caba-ret-style show presented in the theatre on the back of the lot. Westmark closed the lodge in 2013, after making the decision to shuttle holiday package passengers by plane between Fairbanks, Alaska, and Dawson City, Yukon.

Nevertheless, the present owners, Beat and Jyl, have high hopes for their business. It's a large property with many buildings, which hold 174 guest rooms, a restaurant, a bar, three kitchens and staff quarters. The lodge is firmly and immaculately ensconced in 1960s mahogany panelling, and its dining room decor drips with dusty rose, a brown-looking pink that was ubiquitous in the 1980s. A red rotary phone sits in a reception area.

Outside, the grounds are weathered. Walking around the property, one encounters a definitive feeling of abandonment. The landscaping is being overrun by poplars and shrub shoots. There's a well-worn mini-golf course behind one of the buildings, and black ground cloth is peeling up from the soil.

The Ledergerbers keep the business open from May to the end of October. Thirty-two rooms are available during that period, though Beat and Jyl will open rooms in another building for tour groups. Their guests consist of tourists and road crews, and the RV park is one of the busiest parts of their business. Beat says that 2016 was a better year than 2015.

A resident of Beaver Creek since the early 1960s, Beat is deeply invested in his community, having in the past run a garage, truck stop and café, and a sawmill. He remembers the Westmark cabaret shows and the energy that reverberated from the lodge to the rest of the community. He talks of having a show in the theatre, a reason for people to stay for the night, and he's discussing the possibilities with the previous show manager.

For now, the electricity is off in the theatre, a grand log structure behind the hotel buildings. Inside the theatre there's a stage, dining tables, stacks of chairs and a kitchen waiting to cater to large groups. There's a piano where someone has been playing by the light of a thick white candle. This is where Beat's vision comes squintingly into view. He might just pull it off.

7. THE END OF THE LINE

MILE 1225.5 BORDER CITY LODGE & RV PARK TO MILE 1404.1 SILVER FOX ROADHOUSE

Mile 1225.5 Border City Trading Post / **34**
  Border City Lodge & RV Park
Mile 1226 Scotty Creek Services
Mile 1234.5 Seaton Roadhouse
Mile 1260 Lakeview Lodge **35**
Mile 1264 Northway Motel **36**
Mile 1270 Nell Kelly's Roadhouse
Mile 1283 Riverside Lodge
Mile 1306 Forty-Mile Lodge **37**
Mile 1318.5 Tok Lodge **38**
Mile 1338.5 Cathedral Bluffs Lodge / **39**
  Cathedral Creeks B&B
Mile 1361.3 Dot Lake Lodge **40**
Mile 1391.5 Halfway Inn
Mile 1404.1 Silver Fox Roadhouse **41**

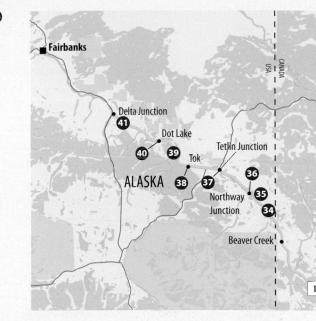

The Canadian government had very little interest in the Yukon Territory in the 1800s. So remote, underpopulated and out-of-mind was the snow-and-ice-covered landmass that Canada (which was ruled as a British colony until July 1867) even missed out on the fire-sale price of purchasing neighbouring Alaska from Russia at $7.2 million in March 1867—not that Russia would have sold Alaska to Britain, its rival from the Crimean War. The Americans weren't convinced of the value of their purchase either and gave it the nickname "Seward's Folly" after William Seward, the man who pushed for and secured the

Opposite: Of all the taxidermy collections at different lodges along the Alaska Highway, the most extraordinary can be found at Mile 1404.1 Silver Fox Roadhouse.

purchase. However, the gold discoveries of the late 1800s and early 1900s, and the oil reserve finds of the twentieth century, would prove the worth of the state.

Canada became a sovereign country in 1867 (British Columbia joined Canadian Confederation in 1871) and wanted to discuss the issue of the boundary of the Alaska Panhandle with the Americans, who simply refused to. The Klondike gold rush of 1897 and the mad rush of thousands of people, the majority of whom were Americans, really put pressure on the two countries to establish a boundary. The Canadians sent half a dozen North-West Mounted Police to the pass of the Chikoot Trail armed with a Maxim machine gun to remind stampeders that they were about to cross an international border and enter Canada. Discussions ensued and failed, but in 1903 an international six-person tribunal consisting of three Americans, two Canadians and one British member decided in favour of the status quo, which is the boundary that exists today. The boundary was later extended in a straight line along the 141st meridian west, marking the divide between Alaska and the Yukon.

MILE 1225.5 BORDER CITY TRADING POST / BORDER CITY LODGE & RV PARK

THE ALASKAN SIDE OF THE Alaska Highway is two hundred miles long, and the first stop once you cross the border is Border City Lodge & RV Park. This lodge started as one of the originals, a trading post owned and operated by the Graheks and mentioned in a 1947 list of highway accommodation. Word has it that Mrs. Grahek was a local woman and that the Graheks traded for furs and crafts with the First Nations people in the region. They grew their business to include a liquor store, fuel, meals and accommodation.

"We were told he got it because he was in the military, and he was disabled and he was given a land allotment, allowed to buy it, or it was given to him," says Neil Deterding, who owns Border City with his wife and business partner, Danielle.

Neil and Danielle make their home in Oklahoma, where they run several companies, but Border City was Neil's first foray into the business world. He bought the lodge from his parents, Wilma and Louis, in 1991, when he was twenty years old. One summer in the mid-1980s, his parents travelled to Alaska and saw that Border City was for sale. Matt Grahek had passed away, and his sisters in the lower forty-eight were selling off his estate.

"My parents bought it in 1986 or 1987," Neil says.

Louis was not a carpenter, electrician or mechanic, and that was

At the young age of twenty, Neil Deterding bought Border City Lodge & RV Park from his parents. That was over two decades ago.

a problem for the Deterdings. The property ran on an ever-temperamental generator and a well, and the lodge itself was in need of a lot of work. "It was more than they could handle. They were in their late fifties and early sixties," Neil says.

The story of how Neil ended up running his parents' lodge has an old-timey quality to it. A man called Bud Marquis, who was known in Alaska for his business dealings in trucking, fuel and the oil pipeline, became friends with the Deterdings. In 1991, Neil spent the summer with his parents at Border City and became Bud's apprentice in business. It was Bud who helped Neil secure a half-a-million-dollar loan from Key Bank (now Wells Fargo) that allowed him to purchase the business from his parents and begin the necessary improvements to the property.

Border City Trading Post appeared in the first, 1949 edition of *The Milepost*, a guide known as the bible of Alaska Highway travel.

"I jumped in with both feet," Neil says. "It needed a new septic, new well. The main building wasn't quite finished and it had a

full foundation that was having some permafrost issues." The work didn't stop there. He cleared the seven-hectare (eighteen-acre) property and installed an RV park, and then remodelled the gas station, café and gift store.

Each winter for the first five years that Neil ran the business, he renovated the lodge. A life operating a frontier lodge wasn't typical for someone Neil's age.

"I did like it, but at first it wasn't very good because of the social life—there wasn't much," he says. For companionship, he'd head southeast across the border. "I spent a lot of time at the Westmark. Beaver Creek was booming because of the Westmark Hotel. We had a lot of fun, a lot of good times, 'cause I could hang out with people my age."

The early 1980s were the peak of the highway lodge businesses; since then, tour bus, RV and tourist traffic has declined. Neil was

faced with the challenge of buying into a business on the downside of that infamous peak. But, in 1996, he was fortunate to meet his future wife, Danielle, and she brought her experience and knowledge of accounting to the business. "She really took off and made the lodge more profitable and efficient," Neil says. "She acquired a lot of debt when she got married—she didn't have much choice."

The new marriage and business partnership brought some changes to Border City. The couple began to acquire local government landscaping maintenance contracts, and with the help of Neil's mentor, Bud, the Deterdings purchased a neighbouring business: "I bought ten acres between United States customs and myself—an old tourism business called First and Last—tore everything down."

For the first five or six years Neil and Danielle ran the business, they closed it down in winter; it just wasn't profitable in the off-season. But once they had the government contracts to supplement the lodge business income, they opened the lodge year round. They ran the business this way for about a decade. Then, once Neil and Danielle started a family, they knew they had to change their work schedule.

Neil and Danielle Deterding have owned Border City Lodge & RV Park for over two decades. Since the couple had children, the family has lived in Oklahoma where they operate several businesses. The lodge is now up for sale. Photo by Lily Gontard.

"We started having kids," Neil said. "School and things for them started being priority." The family managed for a couple of years with Neil leaving earlier in the spring and staying later in the fall to run the lodge. But then they decided to lease it to a long-time employee, Bruce Sorenson, from 2002 to 2013, while the Deterdings built up their lives in Oklahoma.

Neil is the second-youngest of ten siblings, and over the years, many of his nieces and nephews made the journey north to work at Border City. Two of his nephews even considered buying the business from their uncle, but Neil dissuaded his nephews once they had children.

"Their wives had other ideas," Neil says. "They had kids right away, and this [life] isn't nothing if you're having kids."

After being leased to a couple of different leasees, Border City is up for sale. The Deterdings have a caretaker on site who'll keep the lodge and convenience store open for now.

Neil and Danielle have fond memories of their time spent at the lodge, but they've established their lives farther south.

"I never dreamed I'd be where I was at," Neil says. "We enjoyed it until our kids got a certain age."

The fortysomething businessman has some advice for anyone who is looking to take over his lodge. Energy and self-sufficiency are required.

"It's a young man's game," Neil says. "Your work ethic has to be a lot higher."

MILE 1264 NORTHWAY MOTEL AND MILE 1260 LAKEVIEW LODGE

WHEN DALE WILSON AND Clarence ("Pat") Duke met in the 1950s, they probably didn't imagine that their respective children, Lavell and Catherine, would one day hold the distinction of being probably the only married couple in the world whose respective parents each ran lodges along the Alaska Highway. Lavell and Catherine (née Duke) Wilson now make their home in Tok, Alaska, a few miles west of where they first met in 1955, when Catherine's family moved from California to Northway.

In the late 1940s, when Lavell Wilson was on the cusp of adolescence, his father, Dale, who had previously lived in Alaska as a trapper, moved his family from Washington to Alaska.

"Dad was living here in the earlier forties," Lavell says. "He wasn't in the military to start with, but he got drafted while he was up here."

Dale Wilson ran a grocery store, and then he built Northway Motel, which began operating in 1950, with three or four cabins and a gas station. He owned it for about six years, but during that time, he leased it out. Catherine's parents, Pat and Louise Duke, ran the motel for one summer. Don Wilson, Dale's brother, also ran the motel for a short time.

The Dukes staked a sixteen-hectare (forty-acre) trade and manufacturer lease, and opened Mile 1260 Lakeview Lodge in 1961, where they also sold fuel as a Texaco station.

There was almost a decade between the time the Wilsons and the Dukes operated their respective lodges, but both Lavell and Catherine

Opposite: Pat and Louise Duke staked the land where they built Lakeview Lodge and opened it in 1961.

Lakeview Lodge had a series of different owners before falling into ruin.

worked for their parents to varying degrees. When Lavell was a child, he was expected to help around Northway Motel. For Catherine—who was expecting her and Lavell's second child when her parents were running Lakeview Inn—things were a bit different.

"I used to just help out—I never worked there," she says.

Lavell and Catherine have seen a lot of changes in the lodge community over the years. He can list a number of lodges that have opened and closed. "People come up here and think they are going to do something," he says. "Then they find out how rough it is." That point could be made about the life in any rural Alaskan community, but Lavell offers a keen observation about why the people who started the lodge were usually successful, but subsequent owners failed.

"The people who built them [the lodges] would build them slowly," he says. "When they'd sell it, they'd get a lot of money for it. The new owner would spend all their money on buying it, then they couldn't keep going. It very rarely worked out."

Lavell and Catherine Wilson met in 1955, when Catherine's family moved from California to Northway, where Lavell's parents ran Northway Motel. Photo by Lily Gontard.

Although Lavell attended elementary school in Northway, as a teenager he was sent farther afield for high school: to Sheldon Jackson College in Sitka, on the Alaska southeast coast. Originally the college was built in the late 1800s as a "training" school for First Nations children and enforced assimilation of the children into the dominant Christian European culture. By the time Lavell attended the school, it had experienced several changes in governance, had broadened its mandate and was housing children from all over the state. The college closed in 2007.

At the school, Lavell was one of six or seven children from Northway; most of the students were First Nations children from southeast Alaska. "It was a very good school," Lavell says, "but you had to work so many hours a week." He's referring to working in the sawmill or laundromat ten hours a week, something that would be unheard of in modern times.

Despite the fact that their parents had run lodges, neither Catherine nor Lavell was drawn to the lifestyle. "It was a good way to make a living at one time," he says. "With modern highways and cars that go so fast, they don't have to stop every fifty or hundred miles." Even if the traffic slowed, the work remained constant.

"You're working there twenty-four/seven," says Catherine.

"You can't get away from the damn place," adds Lavell.

Alaska was slow to adopt daylight saving time, and until the mid-1950s, this lack of compliance caused some issues for Dale Wilson when he ran Northway Motel.

"There was a couple of times when there was a good three hours between the time in Yukon and Alaska," says Lavell Wilson, Dale's son. "People would pull up at 5 a.m. and be honking the horn, and they're thinking it's like 8 a.m."
—Lavell Wilson, son of Dale Wilson

MILE 1306 FORTY-MILE LODGE

THERE ARE PEOPLE WHO GO to Alaska with lots of romantic notions but no real understanding of what life in the northern bush means. Those are the ones who turn tail and go back where they came from, or die tragic deaths and have movies made and books written about their "adventure." Then there are those people who go in pursuit of their dreams and stay—not only surviving but thriving. Ray and Mabel Scoby and Clarence ("Red") and Freida Post were two couples who fell into the latter category.

Ray and Red were best friends in Michigan, and the pair always talked about moving to Alaska. One day—as Ray's daughter, Jo Ann Henry, tells it—they did just that.

"We moved to Alaska in July 1946," Jo Ann says. "My dad and his

best friend had been talking about it for years—getting out of the rat race in Michigan."

From a twenty-first-century vantage point of immediate gratification, high-speed this and instant that, it's easy enough to giggle at Ray and Red's idea of the "rat race" that they were experiencing in the 1940s. But Ray and Red were living in a post-war era when suburbia was taking hold of the land surrounding the cities, and the United States experienced a burst of economic energy that lasted into the 1970s.

"One day he came home and said we were headed to Alaska," says Jo Ann.

The Scobys packed their sawmill and John Deere tractor and, with the Posts, headed north. It took them one month to travel from Michigan to Alaska. When they reached Dawson Creek, they drove up the Alaska Highway. In Alaska, the two couples saw opportunity in having a roadhouse at the junction of the newly built Alaska Highway and the soon-to-be-built Fortymile Road (now known as the Taylor Highway) that led to the rich gold-mining district of the same name. They applied for a lease on the land at the junction of the two highways before the Fortymile Road was even completed.

First, they had to clear the land of poplars, spruce and aspens, and cut and peel logs for building. This work required all hands, including those of Jo Ann, who was seven at the time, and Jack, her elder brother by two years. ("He's my only, thank goodness," Jo Ann says. "I couldn't handle any more brothers.")

"We hauled moss for insulation," she says. "And I even peeled logs."

Ray was a carpenter who had been working at the American Seating Company in Michigan before moving to Alaska, and he led the construction. His craftsmanship can be seen in the buildings that still stand at Mile 1306, which look surprisingly well preserved. After seventy years, there is hardly a sagging roofline or crooked wall, a fact that speaks to the quality of the original work.

Opposite: The first building the Scobys and Posts built at Forty-Mile Lodge was the café, which is still standing after over sixty years.

The Scobys and Posts started building in 1947, and the restaurant was the first thing they finished. It opened the same year.

"They slowly added all the other buildings," Jo Ann says. "They had a Chevron gas station, nine cabins, four big ones and five little ones."

The early days of Forty-Mile Lodge were challenging for many reasons. Water had to be hauled from Tok until a well was dug at the roadhouse; the children missed one year of school because one hadn't been built yet in Tok; and to buy groceries the entrepreneurs had to drive to Fairbanks, two hundred miles to the west, until a grocery delivery service became available in the area.

"Then they built the big garage, the shower house and the bunk house for the truckers," Jo Ann says. "It was a real going concern."

The roadhouse was open seven days a week, year round. Although

Ray Scoby worked as a carpenter at the American Seating Company and he led the construction of Forty-Mile Lodge.

they operated sixteen hours a day, service was available the remaining eight hours on the honour system.

"We didn't even have a lock on any of the doors. They'd close [the roadhouse] but wouldn't lock anything, and if people came in, they'd go in the restaurant and cook their own meals and leave money on the counter."

The Scobys and Posts were part of a growing community on the Alaskan side of the highway around Tok. That increase in population meant more children, and they needed a school.

"My dad and others built the schoolhouse out of an old road commission barracks," Jo Ann says. "A one-room school, one teacher, all grades."

During the week, Mabel and Freida would take turns driving the children to school. Whoever stayed behind took care of work at the

The Scobys and the Posts moved from the "lower 48" to build Forty-Mile Lodge at the junction of the Alaska Highway and the Top of the World Highway in 1947.

roadhouse. Ray and Red ran the gas station and hired mechanics to work in the garage.

Tok is called the "Sled Dog Capital of Alaska," and the Scoby family took part in establishing that reputation. Ray became known in Alaska to tourists and locals alike for the Siberian huskies he raised at his Shleekai Kennel and the dogsleds he built, which his children used and dog mushers from around the state ran in races. He sold the kennel in 1973, and his dogs are said to be the ancestors of the pups at Alaska Wildwood Siberian Huskies kennel.

"The dogs are probably all over the world now—tourists would stop and buy them," Jo Ann says. "They were beautiful dogs, and I had them all as pets until they were sold. Every time he sold one of those little puppies, I didn't like it one bit."

The Scoby children kept themselves busy with a typical northern occupation, their traplines (they caught squirrels), and they drove their dogsleds. "We were in a few of the little dog races, but when we got old enough, we didn't have time to play—we worked in the restaurant."

For high school, the choices were limited to Fairbanks or somewhere the Scobys had family in the lower forty-eight. Jo Ann and Jack ended up going to Michigan, where they stayed with their Aunt Edna (Ray's sister). Jack went on to university in Fairbanks, and eventually the siblings both ended up back at Forty-Mile with their respective spouses.

"After Jack and I both got married and had a couple of kids, my husband, Lamar, and I moved to Fairbanks in 1965," Jo Ann says. Jack and his wife, Sheila, moved to Anchorage shortly afterwards.

The Scobys and the Posts ran the roadhouse together until around 1955. Then the Scobys bought out the Posts, who moved to the village of Tok, where they ran a gas station and post office opposite the US customs office. The US customs office was located in Tok for many years before it was moved to its present location near the

border. Eventually, the Scobys grew tired of running the roadhouse twenty-four/seven, and they sold it in the mid-1970s.

"My dad could never sit still," Jo Ann says. "He built mini dog-sleds and big dogsleds for those that came for the races in Alaska."

Mabel and Ray built a home and lived in Tok, which has named a street in their honour, until their deaths in the 1980s. Jo Ann and Lamar moved to Georgia, where he was from, and Jack now lives in Arizona, though he makes an annual pilgrimage to Alaska to fish for salmon and halibut.

Jo Ann was last in Alaska in 2008, and she admits that it breaks her heart to see that the roadhouse isn't operating anymore. The doors of the business have been closed since the mid-1980s, but when the Scobys and Posts ran it, they welcomed highway truckers and travellers into their homes every day of the year, including holidays. "My mother was a tough old lady and the truckers loved her."

Jo Ann Henry (née Scoby) has many fond memories of growing up at Forty-Mile Lodge, and it breaks her heart to see how the lodge has fallen into disrepair.

MILE 1318.5 TOK LODGE

TOK IS A THREE-LETTER WORD that elicits giggles, gasps and looks of disbelief the moment it's spoken, but yes, it really is the name of a village in Alaska. How did this settlement—which grew out of a highway construction camp—acquire this odd single-syllable name? Theories abound: one suggests the town was named after a puppy that was a mascot of the 97th Regiment of the US Army Corps of Engineers working on that section of the highway. Another theory says the name was an abbreviation for the city of Tokyo (also a World War II reference); another connects the term to the Tokai River, which is near the village of Tok and is more commonly known as the Tok River. Tok. Now that you're used to it, try this: "Tok

Bud and Pamela Johnson ran Tok Lodge for twenty-eight years. Though they continue to run other service businesses in the community, they have no intention of returning to lodge ownership.

Lodge," which is not code for an adolescent hot-boxing hangout but the name of what until 2004 was one of the oldest operating lodges on the Alaska Highway.

The Tok Lodge Bar sits on the site of the former Tok Lodge, but there is no connection between the two buildings, except the last owner of the lodge, Rory Warren, is the current owner of the bar. In a way, the bar's mock log-rounds siding pays homage to its predecessor: *We shall not forget the good times*.

Tok Lodge was built in 1950 by Lee Evans. Pictures of the lodge show a building that is quite similar in appearance to the Beaver Creek Lodge: a scribed-log, two-storey, rectangular building with tall narrow windows upstairs and square windows downstairs. The lodge housed the first grocery store in Tok and, at one time, the post office.

Tok Lodge burnt to the ground following an early morning fire in 2004. The legendary lodge lives on in the memories of the people who enjoyed its hospitality over the years.
Image courtesy of Bud and Pamela Johnson.

Many old sections of the Alaska Highway have been reduced to dirt roads meandering through the forest.

A few years after he opened the business, Lee Evans died in an accident while clearing land beside the lodge. His widow, Erma, continued to operate the lodge for many years, with Jack Marker as the manager. The full-page ad for Tok Lodge in Lou Jacob's 1957 *Guide to Alaska and the Yukon* boasted of "excellent meals and lunches," "home cooking," "women cooks" and a "cocktail lounge," and noted that the business was open year round. Jacob (who in the introduction to his guide prided himself on listing only the finer establishments) wrote that for a price of eight dollars for either a single or a double, a guest would find that in the lodge "everything is new... and unusually attractive."

Erma eventually sold the lodge, and it would pass through two different sets of hands before it landed, in 1972, with Roy ("Bud") Johnson. By this point, Bud was a long-time resident of Tok, having lived in the town for almost twenty years. In 1955, at the age of nine, he had moved from Missouri to Tok after his parents passed away.

"I was just a kid and came up to live with my brother," Bud says. "He worked for Bureau of Public Roads."

Bud drove north to Alaska with a friend of his brother's. "It was quite an adventure, and it took quite awhile," he says. "When I first got here, the road was gravel from here all the way to Fairbanks. Wasn't very long after that they paved to Delta Junction, then to here."

Bud and his wife, Pamela, met at Tok Lodge and, after "courting" for half a year, the two were married. The couple raised three sons in Tok. Bud and Pamela's lives have been entwined with the growth of the community, and they saw a lot of changes during their twenty-eight years operating the lodge.

"Back then there were a lot of long-haul buses, buses from outside, which, they don't do that now," Bud says. "They fly and travel around. The bus companies at the time were all independents." Tok also suffered, much as did Beaver Creek, Yukon, when the Westmark hotel chain, possibly one of the largest employers and establishments in the community, closed its hotel in 2013.

Like many lodge owners on the highway, the Johnsons started with a lodge, and then grew their business interests from there. They added motel buildings to the lodge and a mini-mart. But you won't catch Bud returning to the lodge business anytime soon.

"I tell my wife, 'If I ever talk about getting back into the food business, shoot me.'"

Tok Lodge survived the transition from owner to owner, the rerouting of the Alaska Highway and a wildfire that came within one mile of the property in 1990. But a fire that started in the kitchen early one December morning in 2004 put an end to the legacy. The building burned quickly, and the heat was so intense, it melted the siding on buildings behind the lodge. Tok residents turned out to watch the end of a legend, which took all of two hours to burn to the ground. One of the oldest lodges on the highway came to a quick and final end. As was the case at the end of many lodges before, not even a sliver of Tok Lodge remains.

MILE 1338.5 CATHEDRAL BLUFFS LODGE/ CATHEDRAL CREEKS B&B

BETWEEN WHERE CATHEDRAL RAPIDS Creek Number 1 and Cathedral Rapids Creek Number 2 flow beneath the smooth-paved Alaska Highway, there is a stretch of the old highway that loops away from the realigned roadway. There, hidden from view, is the Cathedral Creeks B&B, owned by Christa Bentele. At her B&B, she hosts geology field camps and tourists from all over the world. Scattered around her property are remnants of the lodge that operated there from the mid-1950s until the early 1970s: Willy Lou and Marvin Warbelow's Cathedral Bluffs Lodge.

Willy Lou (pictured) and Marvin Warbelow opened Cathedral Bluffs Lodge in the mid-1950s. Marvin based his flying business, Warbelow's Air Ventures, out of the lodge.
Photo courtesy of Cyndie Warbelow-Tack and Art Warbelow.

Willy Lou and Marvin first met when they were both studying teaching at Superior State College, Superior, Wisconsin, in the 1930s. The couple married in 1945, then travelled via steamship up the West Coast to Alaska, and then by railroad into the mainland. The couple spent several years teaching in the remote communities of Shungnak, Unalakleet and Selawik in the Western Arctic before they ended up in the First Nations community of Tetlin, south of Tok.

Cathedral Bluffs had a couple of incarnations before becoming a lodge. It was a highway construction camp and then became, briefly, an Alaska Communications System repeater station.

"Turns out the reception isn't very good out there," says Art Warbelow, the youngest of Willy Lou and Marvin's four children. "It was promptly closed down."

Schooling was a challenge for many families who ran lodges along the Alaska Highway. Years after teaching in remote communities in Alaska, Willy Lou homeschooled the four Warbelow children at Cathedral Bluffs Lodge.

Marvin was an entrepreneur and hard-working scavenger. He developed a reputation as a pioneering bush pilot in Alaska with Warbelow's Air Ventures. There's even a mountain named after him. The three Warbelow sons, Charlie, Ron and Art, turned Warbelow's Air Ventures into 40-Mile Air, which still operates flying services in the region.

Willy Lou was a lifelong teacher, and once she retired, she was a substitute teacher in the Tok school. She became an author and wrote several fiction and non-fiction books based on her time as a teacher in remote communities and her family's experience in the early days of the Alaskan aviation industry.

Marvin Warbelow was a legendary Alaskan bush pilot. He started Warbelow's Air Ventures, which his sons took over after his death. The airline still operates as 40-Mile Air out of Tok, Alaska.
Photo courtesy of Cyndie Warbelow-Tack and Art Warbelow.

"My folks bought Cathedral Bluffs from the government on a sealed bid," says Art. His parents were teaching in Tetlin, and Marvin planned on tearing down the old repeater and highway construction buildings and selling the lumber. "That was back when, as my dad was fond of saying, things were worth more than money in Alaska." When Marvin and Willy Lou arrived at Cathedral Bluffs, they changed their minds.

"There was a real nice house there that could've been only a couple of years old," Art says. "It was built for the commanding officer there. It had hardwood floors, on a poured concrete basement." It was also the nicest-looking house that Willy Lou had ever seen, according to Art. "She told my dad, 'You can't tear that down.'"

The Warbelows had already homesteaded a piece of land east of

Christa Bentele established Cathedral Creeks B&B in 2000. The property was for sale in 2016.

Cathedral Bluffs, and they initially considered moving the house to it, but there was a steel bridge over Yerrick Creek that would have been an obstacle. Instead of moving the house, they abandoned their homestead and moved to Cathedral Bluffs.

By the summer of 1957, the Warbelows had their first guests: a bridge construction crew. "Dad had rented out every building to them, including our house," says Cyndie Warbelow-Tack, the eldest of the Warbelow children. With the lodge fully occupied, the Warbelow family spent the summer living in a twenty-one-foot trailer. That fall, the family headed back to Wisconsin, and in spring of 1958, they returned to Alaska, bringing a plane along with them. "That's when it really became a roadhouse," Cyndie says.

Marvin and Willy Lou valued education, and she homeschooled the children. Ron and Cyndie were a year apart in school, whereas Charlie and Art, who were eighteen months apart, were in the same grade. "The lodge was closed in winter mostly because Mom was teaching us," says Art.

"A lot of people say that we were out of the mainstream because of where we grew up," Cyndie says. But she points out that there was a constant rotation of visitors, many of whom were scientists. "We had biologists, geologists, people doing mapping and research staying there, but Dad was the one who was flying them out."

In fact, in 1960, the Cathedral Bluffs Lodge became the base for the summer fieldwork of the legendary American geologist Helen Foster. Foster is renowned for mapping Japanese territories after World War II during the post-hostilities mapping program, and for her extensive mapping of Alaska, which included the Yukon-Tanana terrane in the central eastern part of the state and the area around Cathedral Bluffs. Whenever Helen stayed at the lodge, she brought graduate students and other scientists with her.

"We were exposed to a lot of interesting people, many who came to Alaska came up the highway," says Cyndie. "But the geologists were a big part of our lives. Helen was almost a third parent for my brothers and me."

By all accounts, the lodge was not a prosperous business. Warbelow's Air Ventures provided the income to support the family. Marvin did a twice-weekly mail run to Tetlin on Tuesday and Saturday, and he would shuttle people between Tetlin and Cathedral Bluffs Lodge, where they could catch a bus to Fairbanks.

The lodge had a restaurant, a store, a gas station and rooms to rent. For one summer, the family even ran a potato chip manufacturing business.

"By the time potato chips got to Alaska, they were powdered or rotten," Art says. "Mom and Dad got a big commercial potato chip machine and bought potatoes, put them in wax paper bags, ironed them shut, and sold them up and down the highway." However, their business didn't survive a second summer, because the batch of potatoes they started off with ended up producing burned and black chips. "They just gave up on it."

To pursue all their endeavours and run the lodge, the Warbelows didn't hire staff outside the family.

"Us kids, we were the labour force," says Art.

"We all pretty much did the same things," adds Cyndie.

The children were paid for the jobs they did, including digging holes for septic tanks and trenches for the waterline from the well to the house, and filling and emptying fuel tanks.

"I remember pumping a fifty-gallon tank of gas into the storage tank, and you got paid a nickel for that," says Cyndie. "In the wintertime, I swept the living room, shook the rugs, three times a week and that was twenty-five cents. So everything had a price on it."

Each of the children kept a notebook in which they tallied what they were owed. "We all had piggy banks, but fairly early on we had savings accounts with banks."

Remnants of Cathedral Bluffs Lodge are scattered about the Cathedral Creeks B&B.

223

And so the entrepreneurial spirit was fostered. But the kids were still kids, and sometimes in the bustle of summer, they made mistakes.

"When I was young, there was a lot of fuel, and handling fuel and barrels," says Art. "Periodically, we'd pump water into the fuel pumps and pump that into a customer's car, they'd drive a couple of miles and the car would quit."

The former gas station office has been repurposed for Cathedral Creeks B&B guest accommodation.

Wrangling the children into work at the lodge extended to helping out with the air service, particularly airplane landings and takeoffs: Marvin used the Alaska Highway for an airstrip, which was illegal at the time.

"When he took off, there were some curves and hills," Art says. "I always think that was why Dad was such a good pilot, 'cause everywhere he landed was crappy. If he was loaded, one of us would run down the road, stop traffic. When he landed, he could see cars and would circle until they were out of the way."

For the landings, one of the children would stand on the road with a dishrag held up so that Marvin could see which way the wind was blowing, while another child would be on the lookout for traffic. "If there was a car there, we'd explain to the driver that there was a plane landing," Art says. "For some people, having an eight- or nine-year-old kid telling people to stop because a plane was landing—this was kind of funny."

The lodge operated as a Chevron gas station, and in the early years, Marvin would drive a flatbed truck loaded with empty fuel barrels to Valdez to pick up fuel and groceries.

After just over a decade of living at Cathedral Bluffs, the Warbelow family was forever changed on May 22, 1970.

"While Dad was in the shop, a paint pot exploded and struck him in the front of his face, and then he fell backwards and hit the back of his head," says Cyndie. After the accident, Marvin remained in a coma until January of the following year, when he passed away.

Cyndie was at university in Michigan at the time of her father's accident, but her brothers and mother were at home. The accident had an effect on all the children's lives. Cyndie moved to Oregon State University to further pursue her post-secondary education and be closer to her father while he was in a nursing home in Seattle. Her brothers took over the aviation business. Willy Lou eventually sold the lodge, and after a series of owners, Christa Bentele bought it, and has operated it as Cathedral Creeks B&B since 2000.

The Warbelow sons remained working in the aviation industry, and even Willy Lou eventually got her pilot's licence, but Cyndie admits to being "firmly planted on the ground." The influence of her parents and Helen Foster shows in Cyndie's biology undergrad and zoology master's. After a stint teaching and running a business with her former husband, Cyndie now runs the Plant Kingdom Greenhouse & Nursery in Fairbanks. Brothers Charlie and Ron have both passed away, but Art and Cyndie live in Fairbanks, where their mother, who turned 101 in August 2016, lives in the Pioneer Home nursing home.

"It was such a huge part of our lives," Cyndie says. "The more time passes, the more I feel we were incredibly fortunate to be raised in a situation like that. We were remote, but our family was close because of that, and we were exposed to many interesting people. We were very, very lucky."

Her brother Art agrees. "We didn't know any better because we didn't live anywhere else, we never went to school, weren't around any other kids," he says. "In retrospect, the most valuable thing that happened to us kids was that we had to work and the homeschooling. All of us went out and started businesses. We worked because that's what our mom and dad did."

Dot Lake Lodge operated for decades in the small community of the same name. After the lodge was closed, the building became a private residence and housed the post office. The property went up for sale in 2016.

MILE 1404.1 SILVER FOX ROADHOUSE

IN 1928, TWENTY-THREE PLAINS BISON (*Bison bison bison*) were transported from the National Bison Range in Moiese, Montana, to the Delta River area in Alaska. The wood bison (*Bison bison athabascae*) were indigenous to the state but had disappeared hundreds of years before. According to the Alaska Department of Fish and Game, there are now close to 1,000 bison in Alaska, and the Delta herd has roughly 450 animals. The herd's spring and summer range is twelve miles southeast of Delta Junction on the Richardson Highway, and then the herd heads northeast, spending fall and winter north of the Alaska Highway before returning to the spring calving grounds. Bison have few predators. Their thick skulls and short necks protect them from the maw of a lunging wolf, and with their herd mentality and swift-hooved ways, bison are alert to the advances of predators, human or animal. Across the border in Canada, the Aishihik wood bison herd in the Yukon has learned to bolt in the opposite direction as soon as the whir of a snowmobile approaches, and the bison weave through trees and among each other as they run—surprisingly quickly. They are difficult animals to hunt.

Every November 1 to December 15, the Alaska Department of Fish and Game takes applications for a hunting tag draw for the Delta herd hunt, which is open from October 1 to March 31. This lottery hunt brings a lot of business to Dan and Eva Splain's Mile 1404.1 Silver Fox Roadhouse, twenty miles east of the northern end of the Alaska Highway.

"The buffalo hunt is probably one of the most unique hunts in Alaska," says Dan, who has operated the roadhouse since 1977. "It's a once-in-a-lifetime hunt. People get pretty excited about it."

Every year, Dan and Eva send a letter to each hunter who has won a tag, explaining the services available at their roadhouse: hunting advice, fuel, cabins, a small store. The Splains also let self-contained hunters park their rigs in the parking lot.

"Most people [hunters] have to plan their vacations around it," Dan says. "We built them cabins because of the buffalo hunt."

The Splains weren't always right out there in the middle of the wintering ground for the Delta herd. Dan is from Pennsylvania and Eva is from the Philippines.

Mile 1404.1 was originally an Alaska Highway construction camp: 18-Mile Camp. "I had an individual who stopped in here, he'd been in that camp," Dan says. "They had tents out here and they stayed in them. After that first winter, they built a bunkhouse and that's now our house."

Fred and Mary Drew bought the property and turned the bunkhouse into the Greenview Inn and Café; Dan bought it from the Drews. Dan had seen the Silver Fox Roadhouse for the first time a few years earlier, in the 1970s. "I was a probation officer, and two guys from Arkansas robbed the place," Dan says. "It was October, the wind was blowing and it was cold, and I thought, *Who the heck would live out here?* Five years later, I bought the place."

The roadhouse is a happy hobby for the Splains, who married in 2004. Eva and Dan both enjoy the lifestyle: fishing, gardening, berry and mushroom picking. With Dan's full-time job as a security guard and an emergency trauma technician for the pipeline on a two-week-on, two-week-off rotation schedule, the couple easily manage to finance their lifestyle as roadhouse owners during the busy hunting season and through the leaner tourism cycles.

"I built the cabins in 1985, and our first customer was a guy on a bicycle, and he stayed in cabin one," Dan says.

The cabins were built by the Splains' neighbour Al Baker, who aside from being a talented carpenter is also one of two taxidermists who've mounted the various trophies in the Splains' taxidermy and knickknacks "museum" adjacent to the shop.

Opposite: Dan and Eva Splain have made a lifestyle out of running their lodge, which is a welcoming combination of quirky decor and down-home hospitality.

"Most people out there, they haven't got a clue what's in here," Dan says. "So when they come in it's just a complete surprise—not your normal gas station."

Lynx, fox and muskox are all on display, along with archival and more recent pictures. At the far end of the building is the Bison Hall of Fame, and its walls are covered with letters and photos of people from their bison hunts. In the centre of the room stands, naturally, a mounted bison.

When Dan bought Silver Fox Roadhouse, the property was running on a generator. In 1980, power lines were strung along the highway, and he plugged in.

"I was at that time on the pipeline working the night shift and invariably the generator would go down when I was on a twelve-hour shift." Dan would come home and find his water pipes and

Greenview Inn and Café (which became Silver Fox Roadhouse) was built on the site of an Alaska Highway construction camp.

house frozen. After he connected to the grid, things were strangely quiet at Silver Fox. "The first couple of nights I'd run out in my shorts 'cause I didn't hear any noise. It took awhile to get used to no noise."

The 1970s and 1980s were a heady time for the highway corridor around Silver Fox Roadhouse: speculation of an oil pipeline, the start and end of a state farming project, connection to the power grid and new regulations for fuel storage for service stations.

In 1988, national regulations regarding fuel storage tanks were developed. Although grants were available, Dan chose the independent route. "I paid for it myself, and it cost $85,000 for one [underground] tank with three compartments," Dan says. "That's almost triple the price of the place when I bought it."

Eva's sister immigrated to the United States and lives with her husband on the Silver Fox Roadhouse property as well. Now, Dan and Eva can take time off and travel in the off season, leaving the roadhouse in capable hands.

When Dan talks about the future of Silver Fox, he becomes excited about a new camera feature on their website that lets people look around the interior of the roadhouse and the cabins. "I had a gal call the other day and reserve for the buffalo. She said her and her husband spent over an hour just looking at stuff—it's kinda unique."

Although the Splains have live-in help to cover the times when they want to travel, they don't want to hire any permanent staff or grow too much. For them, the roadhouse is about having fun, meeting new people and enjoying the interactions with visitors.

"We don't want to get too big, too busy—there are things I should've done or could've done, but I don't want it," Dan says. "I have a life and my wife and we do things together and that's how we like to keep it."

Simple, friendly and a little quirky—all in the tradition of an Alaska Highway lodge.

Silver Fox Roadhouse has an extensive taxidermy exhibit.

AFTERWORD:
THE END, BUT IS IT REALLY *THE END*?

AS MUCH AS THE CONSTRUCTION of the Alaska Highway is a transportation marvel, it remains an inanimate object. However, the human experience of constructing the highway is spiced with heroes, villains, suspense, thrills, successes and disappointments. This is a story that is retold, again and again, from different angles. At every quarter of a century anniversary—the twenty-fifth, the fiftieth, the seventy-fifth—communities along the highway celebrate their roadway lifeline to the outer world.

There is another part of the Alaska Highway story, the one about people who settled along it to run businesses. Lodge owners of the 1940s, such as the Jacquots in Burwash Landing and the Callisons of Toad River, who established the beginnings of the first non–First Nations settlements outside of trading posts along a virtually unroaded corridor. Or the two generations of Porsilds who ran Johnson's Crossing, and the Bradleys, whose extended family operated several lodges over decades between Haines Junction and Beaver Creek, Yukon. It is the previously untold stories of these people that add a greater depth to the highway history. Without the lodge owners, there would not have been services along the highway, and that would have made it virtually impossible to travel on. Yet in 2017, seventy-five years after the construction of the highway, the lodges are a disappearing trade.

These days, investing in an old lodge is an expensive venture because of high fuel prices, as well as changes in health regulations regarding septic fields, wells and, let's not forget, aging underground fuel tanks.

First Nations from Dawson Creek to Big Delta had no say in whether a highway would be ploughed through their traditional territories in 1942. Since then, with the arrival of self-governance and the need for economic development, First Nations governments have reclaimed some properties that have come up for sale. They are looking to the future of their citizens, who have lived for centuries along what is now a highway corridor, and they expect to be living there for many generations to come. It makes sense for them to invest in their traditional territories.

As of the end of September 2016, several Alaska Highway lodges were for sale. The state of the lodges on the market is everything from turnkey—such as Liard Hotsprings Lodge, Buckinghorse River Lodge and Coal River Lodge & RV—to the renovation nightmare that is Cook's Koidern Lodge. Other lodges await a fate yet to be determined, such as the Burwash Landing Resort, which as of September 2016 remained closed to the public and stood on the shore of Kluane Lake, its windows encompassing a breathtaking view.

With 1422 miles of road behind them, travellers can rest up in Delta Junction, the official last stop on the Alaska Highway.

At the time of this writing in late 2016, the Alaska Highway Heritage Society was waiting for the decision on its National Historic Site of Canada designation application for the Alaska Highway corridor. Success could mean renewed historical panel signage, promotion and funding opportunities, as well as preservation of what exists. But, this doesn't necessarily mean that the highway community won't continue to evolve as it is presently: the occasional need for the services but fewer and fewer services to fulfill the need.

Even though a modern-day car may be able to drive the 603 miles between Whitehorse and Fairbanks in one day, that day can get pretty long if somewhere between Haines Junction, Yukon and Tok, Alaska, you lose a tire or blow a gasket. There's nothing lonelier than waiting on the side of the road for a tow truck that may never come.

ACKNOWLEDGEMENTS

THE CREATION OF THE IMAGES held in this book is the result of my visiting places I had never thought to *see* before. I would like to thank my wife, Brooke Alsbury, for travelling all those miles with me and for suggesting that I create a photo essay of the abandoned lodges of the Alaska Highway. Her idea and encouragement led to the creation of my photographic work in this book. In many of these lodges, I had met warm and welcoming lodge keepers in the years since my first drive of the highway so many years ago. Rediscovering their stories, coffee and cinnamon buns was truly my privilege. I would also like to thank the known and anonymous photographers that have been capturing this highway ever since it became a wartime necessity. Special thanks to my son, Seth, and my mother, Heather, who have been patient and good spirited as they accompanied me on the journey.

—Mark Kelly

Throughout the journey that has been the writing of *Beyond Mile Zero*, I have been grateful to be able to access the people who told me their stories, as well as the works of many people who've chronicled their extraordinary lives and the history of the Alaska Highway community: Bob Kjos, *Horseshoe in My Hip Pocket: Lucky Again!*; Ellen Davignon, *Cinnamon Mine: An Alaska Highway Childhood*; Allison Tubman, *The McDonalds: The Lives & Legends of a Kaska Dena Family*; Willy Lou Warbelow, *Head Winds*; Bill Hodson, *Reports from Hines Creek and Coal River*; Daisy Callison, *Mountain Trails*; and Shannon Soucie's biographical notes on her uncle Lash Callison. To borrow from Shaaw Tláa (Kate Carmack) biographer Deb Vanasse,

234

any errors in the retelling of these people's stories are solely mine. Ken Coates's book *North to Alaska!* was an important source of information about both the construction of the highway and the community that sprung up along it, and John Virtue's *The Black Soldiers Who Built the Alaska Highway* was a valuable resource about the role of the racially segregated regiments of the US Army Corps of Engineers in the construction of the highway. I would like to thank KGG for his companionship, love and support during the research and writing of this book.

—Lily Gontard

Mark and I would like to thank our families and friends who were patient and supported us through this project, and at least feigned interest when they had to drive yet another mile "for research" or heard yet another Alaska Highway lodge story. This book would not be possible without the generosity of the people who took the time to share their knowledge or memories of lodges along the Alaska Highway. In alphabetical order: Aksel Porsild, Alaska Highway Heritage Project (particularly Janna Swales, Heather Jones, Sally Robinson, Tascha Morrison and Julie Harris), Allison Tubman, Amanda Harris, Annie and Emmanuel Obeissart, Art Warbelow, Barbara Abbott, Beat and Jyl Ledergerber, Ben and Gail Anderson, Ben Zhu, Beth and George Jacobs, Brian Fidler, Bruce Williams, Bud and Pamela Johnson, Carmen Hinson, Christa Bentele, Chris Winkelmeyer, Craig Boettcher, Cyndie Warbelow-Tack, Dalyce (DesRosiers) Stubenberg, Dan and Eva Splain, Daniel Plamondon and family, Dave Bistransin, David Dickson, David Neufeld, Dennie and Richard Hair, Denis and Linda Bouchard, Don Rutherford and Ryan Hotston, Donna and Brent Rogers, Ellen Davignon (née Porsild), Gay Frocklage (née Simpson), Gordon Steele, Helen and Ollie Wirth, Hilary Bird and Brad Poulter, Howard and Vel Shannon, Jack Gunness, Jessica Parkin, Jim Nelson, Jo Ann Henry (née Scoby), Karla DesRosiers, Kathy Jessup, Ken Coates, Lavell and Catherine (née Duke) Wilson, Lory Dille and Korey Ollenberger, Matthew Lampke, Matthew Roy, Maxine and Bob Kjos, Michael and Janice Williams, Michael Gates, Murray Lundberg, Neil and Danielle Deterding, Netta DesRosiers, Norma White, Olivier and Mylène Le Diuzet, Paul Rivest, Ray Puttonen, Rolf Hougen, Ron Edinger, Ron and Debbie Peck, Ross Peck, Sandy and Frank Ruther, Shannon Soucie, Sid van der Meer, Teena Dickson, Terri Trout, Tetlin Native Corporation, Urs and Marianne Schildknecht, Walter Gutowski, Willy Lou Warbelow and Yukon Archives: Donna Darbyshire, Katherine Bunce, Mario Villeneuve and Shannon Olson.

Many other people have contributed in small and large amounts along the way. Anna Comfort O'Keeffe and the Harbour Publishing/ Lost Moose team, including the invaluable editor Joanna Reid, publicist Nathaniel G. Moore, copy editor Shirarose Wilensky and designer Roger Handling, shepherded this book from a combination of Word files and TIFFs to the paperback you hold in your hands. AnnMarie MacKinnon, associate publisher, and the rest of the *Geist* magazine team published "The Vanishing Roadhouse" in Issue 100, which was our first taste of what the story would look like in print and how it would be received. Marilyn Biderman of Marilyn Biderman Literary Management negotiated on our behalf through book-contract confusion. Freeman Patterson has been a constant and valuable photography mentor, and Jason Wolsky swooped in for emergency Lightroom rescue missions. Special thanks to Lance Goodwin of Icefield Discovery for the roadside assistance with his vintage 1950s Alaska Highway power wagon. And, finally, among the many others who offered encouragement, Michele Genest and Nicholas Graham.

Sorry if we've missed anyone. We did try to keep track.

INDEX

Numbers in **bold** indicate a photograph.

Abbott, Barbara, **13**
Alas/Con Border Lodge, 194
    See also Beaver Creek RV Park
        and Motel
Alaska Highway, **1**, **32**, **201**
    as airstrip, 129–30, 224
    construction of, 20–**21**–24,
        36–37, 54
    construction remnants, **28**, **185**,
        188–89
    "longest main street," 19
    map of, 16–17
    Mile 0, **14**–**15**
    phone access, **130**–31
    public access, 26–27, 37
    flooding (June 2012), 126
Alaska Highway lodges
    construction of, 24, 26, **33**, **36**
    owners, **9**, 13–15
    See also individual businesses
Alaska Highway community, 11–12,
    29–33, 170, 174
    early years, **36**, 68
    decline of, 9, 19, 162, 185, 217,
        232–33
Alaska Military Highway, 20, **27**–29
    See also Alaska Highway
Allinger, Leland, 158
Andrews, Ben and Gail, 29, 60–64
Andrews, Clifford and Loryne, 61–62
Andrews, Gordon, 63

B/A Oil (now Gulf Canada), 116–17
Backe, John and Sally, 147
Bagnall, Lou, 100, 103
Baker, Al, 228
Baskine, Gertrude Tremblay, 27–29,
    31, 133
    guest of Jacquots, 157–58
Bear Creek Lodge, **145**
Bear Flats Lodge, **164**, **182**–83
Beatty, Caulene and Robert, 188

Beaver Creek Lodge. *See* Beaver
    Creek RV Park and Motel
Beaver Creek RV Park and Motel,
    164, 190–**91**–**94**–95, 215
Beaver Creek, 22, 190, 201, 217
Bentele, Christa, 218, **221**, 225
bison, 97, 104, 227–28, 230–31
Boettcher, Adelle and Leonard, 103
Boettcher, Craig, **108**
bonspiels, 12, 19, 90, 162, 174
Border City Lodge & RV Park, **197**,
    198–**99**–**202**–3
Border City Trading Post, **200**
    See also Border City Lodge and
        RV Park
Bouchard, Denis and Linda, **5**, **121**,
    126–27
Boyes, Mr. and Mrs. Arthur, **24**
Bradley, Camilla and Conrad,
    150–51, 172–74, 186
Bradley, Norma. *See* White, Norma
Bradley, Tom, 150–51, 173, 186–87
British Yukon Navigation Company
    (BYNC), 24, 37, 120
Brown, Wes, 50–51
Buckinghorse River Lodge, **35**,
    46–**49**–**51**–52
"Buckshot Betty." *See* Hinson,
    Carmen
buffalo hunt. *See* bison
Burwash Landing, 157
Burwash Landing Resort, 12, 133,
    157–**58**–**59**–62

Callison, Daisy, 80, 121
Callison, Dennis, 81–82, 85
Callison, Dora, 80
Callison, Doris. *See* Simpson, Doris
Callison, Elisha (Lash), 80–82
Callison, Fred, 80, 121
Callison, Gary and Grant, 81
Callison, Marjorie (Marj) (née Clay),
    81–82
Callison, Winnie (née Parker), 81–82
Callison's. *See* Toad River Service

Canada, 197–98
Cathedral Bluffs Lodge, **197**,
    218–**23**–25
Cathedral Creeks B&B, **197**,
    218–**21**–**24**–25
cinnamon buns, 29–**30**, 60–61,
    63, 139
    Ellen Davignon's recipe, 140–41
Clarke, Bob, 83
Coal River Lodge & RV, 30, 32, 37,
    100–**2**–**3**–5
Cook, Dorothy and Jim, 178
Cook's Koidern Lodge, **18**, 24, 120,
    164, 178, **182**
Contact Creek, **94**–**95**, **108**, **111**
Couch, Helen and Orvil, 129

Davie Trail, 67
Davignon, Ellen (née Porsild), 31,
    135–**37**–39, 193
    cinnamon bun recipe, 140–41
Davignon, Phil, 138–39
Davignon, Lise, 139
Davis, Alex, 116
Dawson, George Mercer, 36
Dawson City, 110–11, 71
Dawson Creek, **14**–**15**, 20, 35–37,
    80
Delta Junction, 19, 216, **233**
DeMasters, the, 72–73
DesRosiers, Belle (née Dickson), 114
DesRosiers, Curly, 114
DesRosiers, Dalyce, 119
DesRosiers, John, 114–19
DesRosiers, Karla, 118–20
DesRosiers, Lorn, 120
DesRosiers, Netta (née Zinck),
    114–20
Destruction Bay Lodge, 193
Deterding, Danielle, 199, 202
Deterding, Neil, 199–203
Deterding, Louis and Wilma,
    199–200
Dille, Lory, **44**–45
Dinning, Beverly, 126

Discovery Yukon Lodgings (DYL),
    164, 184–**85**–**87**–**88**–90
    See also White River Lodge
Dot Lake Lodge, **197**, **226**
Double "G" Service, **8**, 31, **66**,
    86–**87**–**92**–93
Drew, Fred and Mary, 228
Dry Creek Lodge, 24, 120
Duensing, Darrell, 158, 160
Duke, Clarence "Pat," 203, 205–6
Duke, Louise, 205–6

Ellis, Cliff, 119
Edinger, Ron, **167**, 170–71
Evans, Erma, 216
Evans, Lee, 215, 216

Fidler, Brian, 97
Fireside Inn, **95**, **106**–7
First Nations, 41, 57, 157, 198
    Aishihik, 146
    Beaver, 36, 67
    Champagne, 146
    Cree, 36, 67
    Fort Nelson, 99
    Kaska Dena, 67–68, 111
    Kluane, 12, 146, 161
    reclaiming land, 232–33
    residential schools, 155–56, 206
    Sekani, 67
    Slavey, 67
    Southern Tutchone, 146
    White River, 190
fishing, commercial, 156–57
Forty-Mile Lodge (Mile 1306), **22**,
    197, 207–**8**–**10**–**13**
Foster, Helen, 222, 225
Frank, Del, 71
Frigon, Ellie, 170
Frigon, Joseph, 166
Frocklage, Gay (née Simpson), 120,
    125–26
Fulton, Bob and Marj, 83

gender roles, 30–31, 124

generators, **101**, 75, 85, 88, **101**, 104, 180
fires, 50–**51**, 86, 188–90
Gloslee, Mr. and Mrs., 186
Grahek family, 198, 199
Greenview Inn and Café. *See* Silver Fox Roadhouse
Gunness, Charlie, 86
Gunness, Jack, 31, 86–**89**–**92**–93

Haines Junction, 11, 145–47
Haines Junction Inn. *See* Kluane Park Inn
Hair, Dennie, 108
Hair, Richard, **108**
Harris, Amanda, **184**–86, 188–90
Henry, Jo Ann (née Scoby), **22**, 207, 209–13
Henry, Lamar, 212–13

Highland Glen, 88, 90
See also Northern Rockies Lodge
Hinson, Carmen (Buckshot Betty), **179**–81
Hotston, Ryan, 38, **40**–43

Iron Creek Lodge, **110**, **112**–**13**

Jac and Mac's Café, 71, 130
Jacquot family, 12, **161**
Eugene (Gene), 157–58
Louis, 157–58
Ruth (née Dickson), 158
Jalufka, Alfred, 22
Joe's Airport (lodge), 26
Johnson, Bud and Pamela, **214**, 216–17
Johnson's Crossing, 29, 31–32, 133–**34**–**38**–43

Kennedy, Mr. and Mrs. B.R., 100
Kjos, Bob, 82–83
Kjos, Maxine, 82–83, 85
Klondike gold rush, 36, 70–71, 110–11, 157, 198

Kluane Community Development Corporation (KCDC),160–61
Kluane Country, 145–46
Kluane Experience, **150**
Kluane Inn, 157–**58**, **161**
See also Burwash Landing Resort
Kluane Lake Lodge, 150, 151–**52**–**53**–57
Kluane Park Inn (KPI), 11, **145**, **147**–**48**–**49**, 161
Kluane Wilderness Village, **164**, 165–**67**–**71**
Koidern Lodge. *See* Cook's Koidern Lodge

Lakeview Lodge, **197**, 203–**4**–**5**–6
Landmark, Betty and Elmer, 86
Landsdell, Jane, 99
Le Diuzet, Mylène and Olivier, **30**, 177–79
Ledergerber, Beat and Jyl, 190–91, 193, 194–95
Liard Lodge, **27**
Liard Hotsprings Lodge, **95**, 97, **98**
Liard River Corridor, 95, 97
Liard River Hot Springs Provincial Park, 97, 99
Little Bart (celebrity bear), 52
Lower Liard River Lodge, **95**–**96**
Lum'n'Abner's, **24**, 26, **35**, **58**–**59**

McCusker, Knox, 54
McDonald family, 67–68
MacDonald River Services, **66**, **76**–**77**
Mackintosh Trading Post, **145**
Marker, Jack, 216
Marquis, Bud, 200, 202
Mazur, Richard, 156
Message Post Lodge, **25**
Mile 351 Steamboat, **34**–**35**, **59**
Mile 1118 Café. *See* Scully's Saloon and Café
Milepost, The, 24, 26, 59, 74, 82, 100, 200

Mogensen, Diane and Jerry, 178, 179–80
Morley River Lodge, **110**, 130–**32**, 193
Mount Kennedy Motel, 151
Mountain View Lodge, 150–54, **164**, 172–**75**–**76**
Muncho Lake, 66, 83, 91
Muncho Lake Tours, 93
Muska, Johnny, 144, 154
Muskwa-Kechika Management Area, 66–68

Noakes, Harry, 56
Northern Alberta Railway, 36, 80
Northern Guides Association, 57
Northway Motel, 203, 205–7
Northwest Highway Maintenance Establishment, 23
Nowlan, Danny, 173, 186

Obeissart, Annie and Emmanuel, 153
Ollenberger, Korey, **44**–45
Olsen, Neil and Sally, 148
O'Rourke, Marilyn and Tim, 96

Parker, Winnie, 80
Peck, Alene, 52–**54**–**55**–57
Peck, Don, 52–**54**–**55**–5
Peck, Patty, Kathy, and Timber, 56
Peck, Ross, 53–57
Pine Valley Bakery and Lodge, **10**–**11**, **30**, **164**, 177–**80**–81
Pine Valley Lodge, **176**, **178**–81
See also Pine Valley Bakery and Lodge
Pine Valley Motel. *See* Pine Valley Bakery and Lodge
Pink Mountain Campsite and RV Park, **35**, **44**–**45**
Porsild, Aksel, 31, 135–**37**–38
Porsild, Ellen. *See* Davignon, Ellen
Porsild, Elly, 31, 133, 135–38
Porsild, Erling, 133

Porsild, Robert (Bob), 31, 32, 133–39, 158, 193
Post, Clarence (Red) and Freida, **22**, 207, 209–13
Pouce Coupe Prairie, 35–36, 80
Price, Bob, 79, 83
Price, Donna, 83
Prophet River Services, **35**, 61
Puttonen, (Trapper) Ray, 97–**98**–99

Quonset hut, **36**, 133, 186

Rancheria Lodge, **5**, 24–25, 37, **120**–**24**–27, 180
Rita's Roadhouse, **13**
Rocky Mountain Lodge, **66**, 72–**73**–**74**–75
Rogers, Brent, 100–**1**–**4**–5
Rogers, Donna, 30, 32, 100–**2**–5
Rover's Inn, 150, **164**, 172–73, 174
Roy, Matthew, **81**, 83–85
Royal Canadian Engineers (RCE), 23
Royal Canadian Mounted Police (RCMP), 75, 186
Ruther, Frank and Sandy, 139, **142**–43
Rutherford, Don, 38, **40**–43
Rutherford, Dorothea, 40

Scoby, Edna, 212
Scoby, Jack, 209–13
Scoby, Mabel, **22**, 207, 209–13
Scoby, Ray, **22**, 207, 209–13
Scoby, Sheila, 212
Scully's Saloon and Café, **164**, 165–**68**–**70**–71
Shannon, Howard and Vel, **46**–50, 51–52
Shannon, Kim and Lance, 48
Shaug, Helen. *See* Wann, Helen
Sheep Mountain Motel, **6**
Shepherd's Christian Society, 38, 40
Shepherd's Inn, The, **35**, **38**–**40**–43

Silver Creek Lodge, 74, **144**–**45**, 150–**53**
  See also Kluane Lake Lodge
Silver Fox Roadhouse, **196**–**97**, 227–**30**–**31**
  See also Greenview Inn and Cafe
Sikanni, Chief, **45**
  See also Pink Mountain Campsite and RV Park
Simpson, Bud and Doris (née Callison), 37, 120–6, 180
Sims, Refines, Jr., 22
Skarat, Caroline (Carrie), 100
Skarat, Gil and Rose, 100
Soldier's Summit, **21**
Sorenson, Bruce, 202
Soucie, Shannon, 80, 82
Southwick, Rocky and Wanda, 83
Splain, Dan and Eva, 227–**29**–31
Steamboat Mountain, **34**–**35**, **59**
Steele, Cliff, 130–31
Steele, Don, 130–31
Steele, Evelyn (née McPhadyen), 127
Steele, Frank, 68–72, 127, 129–31
Steele, Gordon, 70–72, **127**, 129, 130–31
  on the Wanns, 193–94
Steele, Sergeant Sam, 71
Stephan, Gail, 73–74
Stevens, Darrel, 83–85
Summit Lake Lodge, **65**–**66**, 68–**69**–**70**–72
Swift River Lodge, **109**–**10**, 127–**28**–**29**–31, 193

Taylor, Burt, 86
Temporary Foreign Worker Program, 85
Teslin, **110**
Tetsa River Lodge, 29–30, **35**, **60**–**62**–**64**
Toad River, 68, 75
Toad River Lodge, **66**, **78**–**81**–**84**–85

Tok, Alaska, 13, 203, 212–14
Tok Lodge, **197**, 214–**15**–17
Tok Lodge Bar, 215
Transport Café, **110**, **114**–**15**–**17**–20, 125
Trapper Ray's Liard's Hotsprings Lodge, 97–**98**–99
Treliving, Jim, 72
Trout, Don, 166, 170
Trout, John, 165–67, 170
Trout, Liz (formerly Waine), 165–67, 170
Trout, Terri, 165–67
Trutch Lodge, **35**, 52–**53**–**55**–57
Tundra Lodge and RV Park, **13**

US Army
  building of highway, 21–23, 37, 68
  construction camp sites, 19, 50
  Contact Creek, 111
  control of Alaska Military Highway, 28
  Corps of Engineers (USACE), 20, 22

van der Meer, Marilyn, 174
van der Meer, Sid, 12, **172**–75
Village Lodge, The, 73–74

Wann, Clyde, 127, 130–31, 192–94
  Frank Steele friendship, 68–71
Wann, Helen (née Shaug), 71, 193–94
Warbelow, Art, 219–25
Warbelow, Charlie, 220–25
Warbelow, Marvin, 218–**20**–25
Warbelow, Ron, 220–25
Warbelow, Willy Lou, **218**–**19**–25
Warbelow's Air Ventures (now 40-mile Air), **220**, 222, 224, 225
Warbelow-Tack, Cyndie, 221–25
Warren, Rory, 215
Westmark Beaver Creek, 194, 201
Westours Bus Company, 194

White, Norma, 150–51, 159, 173, 186–87
White Pass and Yukon Route (WPYR), 24, 138, 193
White River Lodge, 150, **164**, 173, 184–**88**–**89**
  See also Discovery Yukon Lodgings
Whitehorse, **145**, 155
Williams, Bruce, 154
Williams, Janice, 150–51, 154–57
Williams, Michael, 150–51, 154–57
Williscroft, Walt, 90
Wilson, Catherine (née Duke), 203, 205–**6**–7
Wilson, Dale, 203, 205–7
Wilson, Don, 205
Wilson, Lavell, 203, 205–**6**–7
Winkelmeyer, Chris, 72–**73**–75
Wirth, Ollie and Helen, 11–12, **160**–62
Women Airforce Service Pilots (WASP), 129

Yukon Airways and Exploration, 70, 193

Zhu, Ben, **148**–49
Zhu, Jia Sheng (Gary), 148–49
Zhu, Yue Sheng (Sue), 148–49

Lily Gontard is a writer living in Whitehorse, Yukon, Canada. Her fiction, poetry and non-fiction have appeared in magazines such as *Pushing Out the Boat*, *Geist*, *The Puritan Magazine* and *Cirque*.

Photo Alistair Maitland

Mark Kelly was born in Ontario in 1971. On his eighth birthday he received a Kodak Instamatic 110 camera. He began clicking the shutter then and has not stopped since. His passion for photography has taken him around the world, and after a canoe trip in 1997 to the Yukon, he returned in 1999 to make his home in Whitehorse. Mark splits his time between his counselling practice where he uses photography in the therapeutic process and his personal/professional photographic pursuits. He lives, works and studies with his wife Brooke and son Seth.

Photo Jason Wolsky